COUNTRIES OF THE WORLD

Syria

Gareth Stevens Publishing
A WORLD ALMANAC EDUCATION GROUP COMPANY

About the Author: Patricia Skinner is a British writer who has lived in the Middle East for twenty years and is fluent in Arabic. Her specialty is alternative medicine, but she also writes about a variety of other subjects. She wrote the book on Jordan for this series and *Islam: The Facts*, published by Windstorm Creative in 2004.

Written by
PATRICIA SKINNER

Edited by
MELVIN NEO

Edited in the U.S. by
ERIK GOPEL
BARBARA KIELY MILLER
ALAN WACHTEL

Designed by
JEAN TAN

Picture research by
THOMAS KHOO
JOSHUA ANG

First published in North America in 2005 by
Gareth Stevens Publishing
A World Almanac Education Group Company
330 West Olive Street, Suite 100
Milwaukee, Wisconsin 53212 USA

Please visit our web site at
www.garethstevens.com
For a free color catalog describing
Gareth Stevens Publishing's list of high-quality
books and multimedia programs, call
1-800-542-2595 (USA) or 1-800-387-3178 (Canada)
Gareth Stevens Publishing's fax: (414) 332-3567.

© **MARSHALL CAVENDISH INTERNATIONAL (ASIA) PRIVATE LIMITED 2004**
Originated and designed by
Times Editions Marshall Cavendish
An imprint of Marshall Cavendish International (Asia) Pte Ltd
A member of Times Publishing Limited
Times Centre, 1 New Industrial Road
Singapore 536196
http://www.timesone.com.sg/te

Library of Congress Cataloging-in-Publication Data
Skinner, Patricia, 1956–
Syria / by Patricia Skinner.
p. cm. — (Countries of the world)
Includes bibliographic references and index.
ISBN 0-8368-3118-7 (lib. bdg.)
1. Syria—Juvenile literature.
I. Title. II. Countries of the world (Milwaukee, Wis.)
DS93.S59   2004
956.91—dc22   2004045331

Printed in Singapore

1 2 3 4 5 6 7 8 9 08 07 06 05 04

Contents

AN OVERVIEW OF SYRIA

The area that used to be known as Syria included parts of present-day Jordan, Syria, Lebanon, and Israel. Collectively, they were called the Levant, Greater Syria, or *Bilad al Sham* (bi-LAD uh-SHAM) in Arabic. Syria was part of the Ottoman Empire until its breakup at the end of World War I in 1918. The present boundaries were set over the next several years. The country was run by the French until it became independent in 1946. Since independence, disputes and wars with neighboring countries, an unstable and authoritarian government, and an often harsh environment have left the Syrian people struggling to lead normal lives. Progress has been slow, and today, the Syrian Arab Republic remains far behind its neighbors in terms of economic progress and development.

Opposite: An aerial view of Damascus, the capital city of Syria.

Below: The ancient ruins of the colonnade at Palmyra. The site is located northeast of Damascus.

THE FLAG OF SYRIA

The flag of Syria has horizontal bands of red, white, and black that respectively represent the road to freedom, peace, and the country's colonial history. Two green, five-pointed stars in the middle of the white stripe represent Syria and Egypt and Arab independence. Black, red, and green are the Pan-Arab colors. The present flag of Syria made its first appearance in 1958 as the flag of the United Arab Republic, which was the name of the brief union between Egypt and Syria. It was used as the Syrian flag until the early 1960s and was readopted for use in 1980.

Geography

Located on the eastern end of the Mediterranean Sea, Syria has a short coastline measuring 120 miles (193 km). The rest of the country is surrounded by land. Turkey lies to its north, while to the east and southeast is Iraq. To the south of Syria is Jordan and to the southwest is Israel and Lebanon. Syria occupies a total land area of 71,479 square miles (185,180 square kilometers), inclusive of the Israeli-occupied Golan Heights.

Land

Syria can be divided geographically into the following regions: coastal plain, mountain, steppe, and desert. Most of the people live in the western third of Syria. In the west is a narrow band of land called the coastal plains. Next to the coastal plains is the Jabal an-Nusayriyah mountain range which runs from north to south. The Anti-Lebanon Mountains form the border between Syria and Lebanon. Syria's highest point, Mount Hermon, is part of the Anti-Lebanon Mountains and rises to 9,232 feet (2,814 meters). The country's lowest point is an unnamed location near Lake Tiberias at 656 feet (200 m) below sea level.

GOLAN HEIGHTS

In 1967, Syria lost the Golan Heights to Israel during the Six-Day War. Although the two nations have held a series of peace talks, the future of this territory remains uncertain.
(A Closer Look, page 54)

Below: **Vineyards can be found on the mountain valleys between Hamah and Homs.**

Fifty-eight percent of Syria is covered by the Syrian Desert, which forms a series of undulating plains. The Syrian Desert is a combination of sand desert and rock and gravel steppe. The Syrian Desert extends into surrounding countries, such as Jordan, where it retains its name. In the past, these lands were all part of one country known as Ancient Syria.

Above: **A pedestrian bridge crosses the Euphrates River near Dayr Az Zawr.**

Rivers and Lakes

Syria boasts two large, famous rivers — the Euphrates and the Orontes. The Euphrates is Syria's only navigable river, and it flows from Turkey in the north, through Syria, to Iraq in the southeast. Between 1968 and 1973, a dam was constructed across the Euphrates River at Tabaqah to maximize the potential of Syria's most important water source. The reservoir that formed behind the dam was named Lake Al-Assad. The Orontes River starts in Lebanon and flows north through the mountains into Syria before entering the Mediterranean Sea near Antioch in Turkey. Many dams have been built on the Orontes. They provide hydroelectric power but have had problems, with a major dam collapsing in 2002.

EUPHRATES DAM

In 1968, Syria began building a dam across the Euphrates River at Tabaqah. Starting in 1977, the dam has been used to generate hydroelectric power for use in many parts of the country.

(A Closer Look, page 52)

Climate

A great part of Syria is semi-arid and arid desert. Inland regions can get fairly hot during the summer, especially around Palmyra and the eastern desert areas. Along the coast, summer temperatures rarely rise above 84° Fahrenheit (29° Celsius). Further inland at Damascus, daily mean summer maximum temperatures are between 91° and 99 °F (33° to 37° C). At Palmyra, temperatures range from 99° to 104° F (37° to 40° C), but the area has also seen extremes of 115° F (46° C).

In winter, places further inland, including Damascus and Aleppo, are cold enough to occasionally have sleet and even snow. It is rare, however, for temperatures to fall below freezing except in the mountains. The coastal areas, for example, enjoy a mild winter with temperatures having a daily mean minimum of 50° F (10° C).

Average yearly rainfall varies greatly across Syria with places further inland receiving less. Although the coastal areas have a long dry season that lasts from May to October, they are also the areas that receive the most rainfall. In the mountains and on the coast, the annual rainfall ranges from 30 to 40 inches (762 to 1,016 millimeters), while in the desert, it can measure below 5 inches (127 mm).

DAMASCUS

The capital city of Syria has been home to many different groups of people and remains one of the most important centers of trade for the region.
(A Closer Look, page 48)

Below: **A view of the Golan Heights. The snow-capped mountain in the distance is Mount Hermon, Syria's highest point.**

Left: Still found in Syria, the peregrine falcon is among the fastest animals on earth. Its flying speed has been measured at over 180 miles (289 km) per hour.

Plants and Animals

Syria's varied geography supports many types of plants and animals. This includes 3,150 species of plants, 2,500 species of animals, and 354 species of birds.

The coastal Mediterranean climate is favorable to lemon and orange trees, while yew, lime, and fir trees grow on mountain slopes. The mountains are also home to drought-resistant shrubs, such as boxwood. Although much of the country is desert, twentieth century developments and poor land management have triggered an increase in desertification. This has, in turn, had tragic consequences for the plants and animals of Syria as much of the arable land is stripped of its natural vegetation with the encroaching desertification.

Today, gazelles, wolves, hyenas, foxes, badgers, wild boar, jackals, deer, bears, squirrels, and polecats continue to roam the country, though not in such large numbers as they once did. Syria's indigenous bird life includes the buzzard, falcon, and eagle, but other species of migratory birds also stop at Syria's water holes. The Syrian Desert also supports lizards and chameleons.

In recent years, the greatest impact on Syrian wildlife and plants is an ever-shrinking water supply. As in neighboring countries, Syria's urban development and a growing population have caused a water crisis.

SYRIA'S NATURE RESERVES

As more and more species of plants and animals slowly die out in Syria, caring for the environment is no longer a choice but a necessity. Fortunately, several nature reserves have been established to protect the country's remaining treasures.

(A Closer Look, page 70)

History

Ancient Times

Syria has a history that dates back to about 3500 B.C. Ancient Syria was successively ruled by the Egyptians, Babylonians, Hittites, Assyrians, Chaldeans, and Persians. It became part of Alexander the Great's empire in 333 B.C. It was later a province of the Roman Empire and then a province of the Byzantine Empire. In the seventh century A.D., the Arab Muslims became the new rulers of Syria.

Ancient Cities

Palmyra, situated in central Syria, has always been a center of trade. Between 1000 B.C. and 900 B.C., it was an Assyrian caravan town. Later, it became an important outpost of the Greek Empire for two hundred years. Under Roman rule, a period of prosperity took place, a result of taxing the caravan trade passing through the area. In 1089, Palmyra was destroyed by an earthquake.

SYRIA'S ROLE ON THE SILK ROAD

For thousands of years from the first century B.C. to the fifteenth-century A.D., the ancient Silk Road linked major trading cities in Europe, the Far East, Africa, and the Middle East. Antioch (called Antikiya and located in Turkey today) was an important Syrian city along the route. The city became prosperous from the caravan trade to India. Many different goods were traded on the Silk Road. Although few traders traveled its entire length, goods were traded at destinations far from their origin.

QUEEN OF PALMYRA

Ancient Palmyra had several notable rulers. The most flamboyant of these was the Warrior Queen Zenobia who ruled from A.D. 267 to 272. (*A Closer Look, page 66*)

Left: Syria's many ancient sites provide archaeologists with valuable clues about early civilizations. This triumphal arch, dating from Roman times in the first century A.D., still stands at Palmyra.

Left: An illustration of the city of Antioch, which was located along the major trade routes of that time.

The End of Ottoman Rule

By the time of World War I, the area that is present-day Syria had been part of the Ottoman Empire for four hundred years . Events in this region, which briefly gained independence during this time of political unrest, played an important role in the fall of the Ottoman Empire.

As a part of the war against the Ottoman Turks — and to strengthen their position in the Middle East compared to that of France — the British encouraged an Arab revolt. The British asked Sherif Hussein, the leader of the Hashemite family, to help the Arab revolt, giving him assurances that the Arab leader took as a promise of power and kingship once the Ottoman Empire was defeated. Arab nationalists also wanted the Hashemites to rule, so on June 5, 1916, the tribes of the Hijaz, led by the sons of Sherif Hussein and advised by British officers, staged a revolt against the Ottoman Turks. After a fierce struggle, one of Hussein's sons, Faisal, entered Damascus as a hero in October 1918.

Faisal, as military governor, assumed control of all of Syria except for areas along the Mediterranean coast in which French troops remained. In July 1919, Emir Faisal convened the General Syrian Congress, which declared Syria sovereign and free. In March 1920, the congress proclaimed Faisal king of Syria. King Faisal started the reconstruction of Syria, declaring Arabic the country's official language, reopening schools, founding new schools, and appointing a committee to begin writing a constitution for Syria.

AN INFLUENTIAL LEADER

Khalid Ibn al-Walid, who lived in the seventh century A.D., was a Muslim who led a number of missions to spread the Islamic religion. He spent the last seven years of his life in Homs. Hundreds of years after his death, a beautiful mosque was built in his honor.

(A Closer Look, page 58)

CRAC DES CHEVALIERS

Built in the twelfth century, this crusader castle lies near the city of Homs and is one of the best surviving buildings of its kind.

(A Closer Look, page 46)

After World War I

Several political forces combined to make Faisal's kingdom short lived. During World War I, Britain, France, Italy, and Russia had met to decide how the Ottoman Empire would be divided. Britain wanted to keep control of eastern Mesopotamia in order to prevent Russian influence in the region from growing and to protect its oil interests. France was also determined to remain a power in the Middle East. After the Russian Revolution, the Russians published documents showing that apparently conflicting promises and agreements had been made. Under the Sykes-Picot Agreement of 1916 — which was signed only six months after Britain had won Hussein's support for an Arab revolt by making what the Arab leader thought were promises for an Arab kingdom — Britain agreed to give France control of the area that became Syria. In addition, although Britain had promised to recognize an independent Arab state under the Sykes-Picot Agreement, it had also promised, in the Balfour Declaration of 1917, to support a Jewish state in Palestine, an area that Arabs considered theirs.

Below: **Although the Arab states in the Middle East wanted to be independent, their request was ignored by world leaders meeting at the 1919 Versailles Peace Conference.**

Above: **This mural depicts Arabs fighting against the French in the twentieth century.**

At the 1919 Versailles Peace Conference, U.S. president Woodrow Wilson asked that Arab claims to independence be given consideration. Faisal represented the Arabs. The pleas fell on deaf ears, and in the end, Faisal returned to Damascus and declared Syria independent anyway.

This independence was not recognized by France and Britain. At the Supreme Allied Council meeting in April 1920, the Arab states were partitioned according to the Sykes-Picot agreement. France was given a mandate to rule Syria, and French forces marched into Damascus, crushing all Arab resistance. On July 25, 1920, Damascus was taken by the French. Faisal fled to Europe.

Modern Times

Although it was ruled under a French mandate as an independent republic after World War I, true independence for Syria was still a long way off. When France fell in 1940, Syria was for a short time administered by the Vichy regime, a Nazi-controlled group that held power in part of France during World War II, until it was retaken by Free French and Arab forces in 1941. During World War II, Syria was an Allied base. Syria finally achieved full independence in 1946. It became part of the United Arab Republic when it joined with Egypt between 1958 and 1961. In 1961, Syria achieved independence for a third time following a revolution.

THE BAATH PARTY
The Baath Party had its beginnings in a political organization formed in Damascus in 1943. The party advocates the formation of an Arab nationalist movement that is free from Western ideas. The party has two main sections. One forms the ruling party of present-day Syria that came to power in 1963. The other branch used to be the ruling party of Iraq when it was led by Saddam Hussein.

Hafez al-Assad

In November 1970, Hafez al-Assad, a Baathist and former defense minister, led a successful coup. He became president of Syria in March 1971 and stayed in power for twenty-nine years until his death in 2000. During Hafez's rule, Syrian foreign policy was based on the goal of regaining the Golan Heights from Israel and preventing Israeli advances. Hafez maintained that the Arabs needed to unite to regain their lost land. This was a reason for his efforts to build ties with the rest of the Arab world.

A New Era

Upon Hafez al-Assad's death, his son Bashar al-Assad became president. Bashar was never the intended heir, and it was only upon the death of his older brother that Bashar's training began. President Hafez and his supporters tried their best to pave the way to leadership for Bashar, and the Syrian constitution was even amended to allow Bashar to stand for election. Bashar ran unopposed, and he was sworn in as Syria's president on July 17, 2000.

Above: **President Bashar al-Assad has not been very successful in improving Syria's economy despite the adoption of many Western methods. The challenge will be for him to accomplish much more before his term is up in 2007.**

Left: **Posters of President Hafez al-Assad are found all over Syria. In 1973, he and Egyptian president Anwar Sadat led their countries in an attack against Israel in the Yom Kippur War. Both of their armies were beaten back. Israel returned the territory it gained from Syria during this war, but it remains in control of the Golan Heights.**

Alexander the Great

In 333 B.C., the army of Alexander the Great defeated Darius III, a Persian king, in the battle of Issus in northern Syria. By 332 B.C., Alexander had full control over the region. Although Alexander died in 323 B.C., Greek culture exerted great influence over the area. The Greek language was spoken, Greek art and architecture almost totally eclipsed the local traditions, and Greek learning and philosophies even became the norm.

Jamal Pasha (1872–1922)

A military leader and commander of the Ottoman army, Jamal Pasha suppressed the rising tide of opposition to Ottoman rule by Arab intellectuals. Also called Jamal the Butcher, one of his orders was the execution of a number of Syrian opposition leaders on May 6, 1916. Modern Syria remembers this day as Martyr's Day, a public holiday.

Alexander the Great

Adib Shishakli (1909–1964)

A Syrian army officer, Colonel Adib Shishakli served with the French army and later fought against the Israelis in the 1948 Arab-Israeli war. He led two coups against the government in December 1948 and November 1951. In July 1953, the Syrians approved a new constitution making Syria a republic, and Shishakli was elected president. By the end of 1953, Shishakli's regime, which had become a dictatorship, started to collapsed. On February 25, 1954, the army staged Syria's fourth coup and restored the 1949 government. Shishakli was forced to resign and left for Brazil on February 25, 1954.

Asma al-Assad

Daughter of a wealthy Syrian businessman, Asma attended school in Britain. She gave up her career as a financial analyst to marry Bashar al-Assad who later became president of Syria. Asma has taken an active role in politics and social and humanitarian issues. In November 2001, she attended the first summit of Arab first ladies, held in Cairo. She is also one of the first Syrian first ladies to accompany her husband on state visits.

Asma al-Assad

Government and the Economy

The Syrian government is made up of three branches: executive, legislative, and judicial. The head of the executive branch is the president. Bashar al-Assad was sworn in as Syria's sixteenth head of state on July 17, 2000, for a seven-year term. Syria's president is also commander-in-chief of its armed forces. President Bashar is assisted by two vice presidents, a prime minister, three deputy prime ministers, and a council of ministers called a cabinet. All of these positions are appointed by the president.

The legislative branch consists of a unicameral People's Council known as the *Majlis al-Shaab* (MAJ-lis a-SHAAB). There are 250 members in the council, and they are elected by the people for four-year terms. Council elections were last held in March 2003. Since 1963, power in the Syrian government has been held by the Baath Party. Under the constitution, the Baath Party is guaranteed 50 percent of the seats in the council.

Below: **Syrian Defense Minister Mustafa Tlass was sworn in as a member of the cabinet by President Hafez al-Assad on March 20, 2000.**

The judicial system in Syria is based on both Islamic law and a civil law system. There are several types of courts in Syria. Civil and penal cases are heard by Summary Courts, and the First Instance Court handles criminal cases. There are also special religious courts that try people according to Islamic law. The highest court is the Supreme Constitutional Court. Its justices are appointed by the president to serve four-year terms.

The Syrian Arab Republic appears to be ruled in a democratic manner. In reality, the president has almost complete authority. Furthermore, because there is not another candidate in elections, the president is not held accountable to the people of Syria.

Local Government

The country is divided into 13 provinces: Al-Hasakah, Al-Ladhiqiyah, Al-Qunaytirah, Ar Raqqah, As Suwayda', Dar'a, Dayr az Zawr, Dimashq, Halab, Hamah, Homs, Idlib, and Tartus. A province or administrative unit is called a *muhafazah* (mu-HAF-az-ah). Each muhafazah is headed by a governor who is nominated by the Minister of the Interior and appointed by the cabinet. The governor of each muhafazah rules with the assistance of a provincial council. Members of the provincial council are elected by the people.

Below: Policemen and other local officials maintain law and order in Syria's cities.

Economy

In the past, Syria was considered primarily an agricultural nation, although the country's industries also include food processing and textile production. Most people were employed as farmers who cultivated crops and raised cattle. In recent years, the government has initiated a policy of industrialization that has changed the economic structure of the nation. Oil plays an important role in Syria's economy with revenue from the petroleum industry accounting for about 65 percent of the country's exports in the late 1990s. The agricultural sector remains important, and in 2002, it accounted for 27 percent of Syria's Gross Domestic Product (GDP) and employed 23 percent of the workforce.

Agriculture and Natural Resources

Syria's main crops are cotton, wheat, potatoes, olives, chickpeas, and lentils. A wide variety of fruits and vegetables is also grown. Until the oil boom of the 1970s occurred, cotton accounted for over one-third of Syria's income from exports. It still totals 50 per cent of crop production. Unfortunately, overirrigation and flooding have increased the salinity in the soil, and unless properly treated, the land may be unsuitable for further agricultural use. Much of the land around the Euphrates has already become infertile.

SOUKS

A popular attraction in Syria are its souks, or covered markets, that were built during the Ottoman era. The busiest souks are in the cities of Damascus and Aleppo. Each souk has a different atmosphere and offers one craft or type of merchandise, such as brocade, embroidery, engraved copperwork, hand-blown glass, silver, gold, or spices.

NORIAS OF HAMAH

Norias, or giant water wheels, were built in the city of Hamah along the Orontes River to supply water for domestic use and irrigation.
(A Closer Look, page 62)

Left: The agricultural industry is heavily dependant on manual labor. Much of the harvesting is still done by hand. These women are employed to pick cotton in the fields.

Left: **Syrian Oil Minister Maher Jamal (*right*) visits the booth of Dutch oil company Shell at the 2000 Damascus Oil Fair, which was jointly organized by the Syrian oil ministry and international oil companies.**

Soil exhaustion is another serious problem because farmers are too poor to rotate crops and manage their land properly. Fortunately, the Syrian Ministry for Agriculture and Agrarian Reform has taken steps to improve the state of affairs for farmers.

Syria's main natural resources are petroleum, natural gas, phosphates, and rock salt. Deposits of iron ore, chrome and manganese ore, asphalt, marble, and gypsum are also found.

Trade

Syria's main export partners are Germany, Italy, Turkey, and France. Major exports include crude oil, petroleum products, fruits, vegetables, and cotton. The main imports are machinery and transportation equipment, food, livestock, and metal and metal products. Some of Syria's import partners are Italy, Germany, France, Lebanon, and South Korea. Since Syria's imports greatly exceed exports, there is a trade imbalance, meaning the country spends more than it earns, causing the economy to be stagnant.

Transportation

The main provinces and cities in Syria are connected by a network of highways and roads. The country has two international airports at Damascus and Aleppo. There are ports in Latakia and Tartus, and railroads connect the main cities and bordering countries.

People and Lifestyle

For thousands of years, the Middle East was largely dominated by nomadic or Bedouin tribes. This tradition has largely faded, and tribal groups comprise only a small percentage of Syrian society today. There still exist a few tribes, but it is estimated they make up less than 7 percent of Syria's population. These nomadic tribes remain semi-autonomous, living primarily in accordance with their own customs rather than those of the rest of Syrian society.

The largest remaining Syrian tribe is the Ruwala. Next is the Hassana of the Syrian Desert. The Butainat and the Abadah come from the area around Palmyra. The Fadan Walad and the Fadan Kharsah come from the Euphrates Desert, and the Shammar az Zur and Shammar al Kharsah come from Dayr Az Zawr province.

Demographics

In 2002, Syria had a population of about 17.6 million. About 90 percent of the people are of Arab descent, including about 391,000 Palestinian refugees. In 1967, when Israel occupied the Golan Heights, many people living there also moved to other cities in Syria.

Below: **Some Arabs still lead a traditional nomadic lifestyle. These herdsmen tend their sheep on the outskirts of the city of Hamah.**

Family Life

Syrian family life is dominated, for the most part, by its Islamic heritage. Families are close, and the bonds are held by strong family traditions based on and molded by Islam. Respect for parents is a feature of Syrian family life, and children are taught to have a strong sense of respect for their elders. Following the teachings of Islam, women dress modestly, keeping most parts of their bodies covered. The diet of many Syrians also follows Islamic principles, and they refrain from eating pork or drinking alcohol. Muslims are required to pray five times a day, so activities are often planned around these prayer times.

Life revolves around the extended family, and a person's devotion to his family takes precedent over all else. A Syrian's honor and dignity are tied to the good reputation of his family and, in particular, the women in the family. For this reason, although strict seclusion is no longer enforced, contact between the sexes is largely limited to that of close family members.

Syrian families are clearly patriarchal; however, Islam teaches that it is a woman's duty to raise the children and manage the household. Although women play a larger role domestically, men are still the authority at home and are more dominant in the workplace.

Above: **Many Syrians spend their free time with family members. These women and children pose for a picture while on a family outing.**

Syrian Weddings

Social events are opportunities for family and friends to get together and enjoy themselves. For this reason, many Syrians look forward to being invited to attend a wedding ceremony.

The first step toward a Syrian wedding is for the groom's family to formally ask for the bride's hand in marriage. There is a first ceremony at which the wedding contract is signed. Although the bride and groom are now legally man and wife, they will continue to live in their parents' homes. The second party is the actual wedding, and it is usually held a few weeks or months later. This ceremony is often followed by a honeymoon.

During the wedding party, men and women sit in different halls. The groom sits next to his bride in the women's party for a while. There, they will have a cake cutting ceremony followed by the gold ceremony, during which the groom formally presents his bride with all the gold that he and his family have brought as part of the *mahr* (MAR), or bride price. The groom is assisted by his mother or another close female relative, with the bride's mother standing nearby. Following tradition, the groom actually places the pieces of gold on his bride. This is a glittering procedure, and the women gather around to see what the bride receives.

Above: A Syrian couple dressed in traditional wedding attire. In Syria, it is common for marriages to be arranged by the parents who try to pick a suitable partner for their son or daughter. Although divorce is allowed under Islam and Syrian law, only about 7 percent of marriages end in divorce. In the case of a divorce, a woman can return to her family's home, where she will be well taken care of. She may also live with an adult son.

22

Women in Syria

Although a number of Syrian women now work outside the home, the number remains low and was only 28 percent of the work force in 1998. Many women still hold the traditional roles of wives and mothers.

Syria has developed its own customs, many of which oppose those of Islam. For example, in many rural areas, women are not allowed to inherit or own property. Muslim women, however, were given these two rights when Islam was founded. In this respect, the plight of women in rural Syria seems to be worse than that of women in surrounding countries. Although recent laws in the country now accord Syrian women the same legal rights as men, in many instances the law is not enforced.

Syrian women are gradually taking on a greater role in the country's affairs. In 1973, during the first session of the Syrian People's Council, there were five female members. This number has increased over the years, and in early 2004, there were thirty female members.

Below: **In 1967, the General Union of Syrian Women was set up to encourage women to take a more active role in society. The women below work outside the home in the agricultural sector, picking onions.**

Education

The Syrian education system consists of three stages of schooling. All Syrian children between the ages of six and twelve must attend six years of primary education. The second stage of schooling lasts for three years and is called intermediate or lower secondary school. At the end of these three years, students take an exam. The results of this exam determine whether their course of study for the three years of upper secondary education will be either an academic or vocational program. Based on their performance in secondary school, students may then attend a university or a technical college.

The Syrian school curriculum includes Arabic, which is the language of instruction. From the age of eight, children must study a second language, such as French or English.

Over the past couple of decades there has been an increased demand for education. In response, more secondary schools and universities have opened. The government is pursuing a vigorous literacy program, and during the 2001/2002 school year, over 4.3 million Syrian children were enrolled in full-time studies.

Below: Syrian children on their way to elementary school. Based on 2003 statistics, the average literacy rate of Syrians aged fifteen and older is 76.9 percent. The literacy figure is higher for males (89.7 percent) than that for females (64 percent). One reason for this difference is that many females living in rural areas do not attend school.

Higher Education

Syria has four universities: Aleppo University and Damascus University, which are the two main universities, Al-Baath University in Homs, and Tishreen University in Latakia. In addition, there are other institutions of higher learning and a number of technical colleges. Vocational programs take three years to complete, while a bachelor's degree requires four to six years depending on the course of study. The highest degree obtainable in Syria is a doctoral degree. The tuition at Syrian universities is low. Many students, however, prefer to attend colleges and universities in other countries if they can afford to.

Syrian Ministries for Higher Education

Three national bodies, the Ministry of Education, the Ministry of Higher Education, and the Council of Higher Education, are responsible for the administration of the Syrian education system. They supervise the training of teachers and tightly control the curriculum. This control has resulted in a higher literacy rate. It has also allowed the national government to limit the available educational programs to those that will produce the type of workers most needed by Syria.

Religion

About 90 percent of Syrians are Muslims, or followers of Islam. The remaining 10 percent of the people are Christians. There are probably less than one hundred Jews in the country. Since Syria is predominantly Muslim, the call to prayer from the mosques, which occurs five times a day, can be heard all over the country. Islamic law is called *shari'a* (shah-REE-ah) and has rules for all aspects of life. These rules are part of the Syrian legal system.

There are different Muslim sects in Syria. Sunni Muslims represent about 74 percent of the population. Other Muslim groups include Shi'ites, Alawites, and Druzes. These different groups live harmoniously and get along with each other. Sometimes, members of these groups even intermarry. For example, President Bashar al-Assad is from an Alawite family, and his wife is from a Sunni family.

Historically, non-Muslim religious minorities coexisted peacefully with Muslims. From the Ottoman Empire onward, non-Muslims were accorded the same rights and legal privileges that Muslims enjoyed as long as they paid taxes. Non-Muslims were able to maintain their own religious practices provided they did not try to convert Muslims to their faith. In 1947, Jews in Syria

OMAYYAD MOSQUE

The Omayyad Mosque in Damascus was built in A.D. 705. Over time, it has become an architectural prototype for hundreds of mosques throughout the Islamic world.

(*A Closer Look*, page 64)

Below: **Just like other Muslim men around the world, these Muslim men in Aleppo visit the mosque to pray on Fridays.**

26

faced persecution as a result of the United Nations decision on Palestine, and many of them left the country. The government of Syria kept a close watch on Jews in the country, and only in 1992 were most restrictions on them, including emigration, lifted.

Muslims make God, or Allah, central to all aspects of their daily life. Every act is initiated with the words *bismillah* (bis-ME-lah) which means "in the name of God" to ensure that all of a person's daily acts are aided by the will of Allah.

All Muslims must follow five tenets, or principles: pray five times a day; donate money to the poor; fast during the holy Muslim month of Ramadan; make a pilgrimage to the holiest Islamic city, Mecca in Saudi Arabia; and recite the *shahada* (shah-HAH-dah), a prayer that professes their belief that there is no god but Allah and that Muhammad is Allah's prophet.

Although Christians are a minority in Syria, Damascus has been the site of significant events in the history of Christianity. St. Paul taught the people in the city about Christianity and faced persecution. He escaped by being lowered in a basket from a church window. The head of St. John the Baptist is also believed to be in a tomb in the Omayyad Mosque, which was once a cathedral. Christians in Syria worship in Roman Catholic churches, Orthodox churches, or Protestant churches. Today, most of Syria's Christians live in Damascus and Aleppo.

Above: **Syrians have the freedom to practice the religion of their choice. These men recite their prayers in a Syriac Catholic rite at the Deir Mar Moussa Monastry.**

Language and Literature

Arabic is the official language of Syria. French is often spoken in the cities and is also used in business communications. The French language is a legacy of the French occupation of Syria, which lasted from 1920 to 1946. Syrian children also understand French or English as they are required to learn a second language while in school. The people of Syria also speak a variety of other languages, including Kurdish, Armenian, Aramaic, and Circassian.

Although a number of newspapers are published in Syria, there is no freedom of the press, because newspapers are often under direct government control. Even local magazines and journals are run by official or semi-official government bodies.

Syrians have contributed to Arabic literature and have a proud tradition of oral and written poetry. Some Syrian poets and writers have become widely known in the Middle East for their work.

Most modern Syrian writers have become well known because of their willingness to speak out on political and cultural issues. These writers have used literature to express themselves

Below: **Street signs in Damascus, as in other Syrian cities, are mainly written in Arabic, although some English words may also be included.**

regarding the oppression and hardships that have affected their lives since the end of World War I. These writings have landed many poets, writers, and members of the press in prison.

Hani al-Raheb (1939–2000)

Born in Latakia, Hani al-Raheb quickly wrote his first book, *al Mahzoumoun*, when he was just twenty-two to try and win a magazine prize. His other novels focused on such issues as the Arab identity, culture, and future. Due to his radical comments and portrayal of the Syrian political situation, he was expelled from his teaching post at Damascus University and twice from the Arab Writers Union. Upon his death in 2000, however, he was eulogized by both the Syrian Ministry of Culture and the Arab Writers Union.

Nihad Sirees (1950–)

A civil engineer by training, Nihad Sirees was one of the first Syrian writers to depict Syrian society in a historical novel. Born in Aleppo in 1950, Sirees's novel *The North Winds* attracted wide acclaim. He has also written plays, and his television drama, *The Silk Market*, was also a first in that it depicted the reality of life in Aleppo on Syrian television.

UGARIT
Ugarit is an ancient city north of Latakia on the Mediterranean coast. Clay tablets dating from the fourteenth century B.C. and inscribed with an early form of the alphabet were discovered there.
(A Closer Look, page 72)

Arts

Syria has long been a center for crafts that are both practical and stunningly beautiful. Not surprisingly, Syrian crafts have been much sought after throughout the world for centuries.

Fabric and Embroidery

Silk damask, a luxurious cloth that is used to make bed sheets and table cloths, originated in Damascus. Expensive gold brocade also has its origins in Syria. These two fabrics are closely associated with Syrian weaving tradition.

Many Syrian women are highly talented at embroidery, and they produce beautiful garments for the fashion industry. Both luxurious and simple fabrics become sought-after items with the addition of embroidery and are used to create elegant gowns and jackets. Home furnishings, such as cushions, also feature embroidery. Designs are complicated and often include flowers, trees, and other signs of nature or repeated geometric patterns.

DEAD CITIES OF ALEPPO

Established many centuries ago, Aleppo has a rich history and is Syria's second-largest city. Today, it is a thriving center for commerce and industry.
(A Closer Look, page 50)

Left: **A clothes shop at a souk in Aleppo showcases a selection of fabrics and embroidery for which Syria is famous.**

Syrian Metalwork

Metalwork has been popular across the Middle East for centuries, and Syrian craftsmen are acknowledged throughout the region for the excellence of their craft. They produce outstanding works in brass, copper, silver, and gold.

Items created in Syria include trays, water flasks, incense burners, trinket boxes, and coffee pots with little cups to match. Traditional Syrian metalwork also includes weapons, such as flintlock pistols and daggers of various designs. Many examples of this work are either brass with silver inlays or pure silver.

Intarsia

Another craft for which Syria is famous is woodwork intarsia. Intarsia is the art of inserting small, intricate, mosaic-like pieces of mother-of-pearl and bone into pieces of wood to make elaborate designs. Examples of Syrian intarsia from the tenth century show art of a highly developed stage. Syrian woodwork items that usually have intarsia are coffee tables and side tables, trinket boxes, Quran stands (used when reciting the Quran), and large storage chests.

Above: **A craftsman at the Artisan Center in Damascus adds the finishing touch to a decorative ceiling panel.**

NIELLO

Syrian craftsmen specialize in producing a decorative treatment for silver called niello. For this effect, a powder made of silver, copper, lead, and sulfur is applied to engraved metal and heated. The heat causes the black powder to melt and fill the engraved areas, creating a decorative effect of black and silver.

An Ancient Heritage

Archaeologists in Syria have discovered extensive writings and evidence of a vibrant, flourishing culture in and around the ancient Syrian city of Ebla. Throughout Syria, there is also evidence of a rich artistic heritage as found in the ruins of ancient classical cities, such as Aleppo and Bosra. Archaeological work has also uncovered numerous relics and artifacts left by the Roman and Byzantine Empires and later by the Muslim caliphs.

Art & Architecture

Syria is a nation particularly fond of the arts, and there are a number of prominent Syrian artists. A few of the most successful painters include Ikbal Karisly (1925–1969), Louai Kayyali (1934–1978), and May Abou Jeib (1974–). The country has also had many talented craftsmen who have been able to design and build beautiful homes. For generations, these craftsmen have wandered around the country making good use of their skills. A typical Syrian home has rooms organized around one or more courtyards. The courtyards are beautifully landscaped with plants and flowers, and many even include fountains that provide a soothing effect. Today, people in the city often live in apartments instead of houses, because apartments make better use of the land.

BOSRA

Bosra is one of Syria's most ancient cities. One of its best-preserved ruins is the famous Roman Theater, built in the second century A.D. The theater, which seats fifteen thousand spectators, is remarkable because it is completely freestanding.

(A Closer Look, page 44)

Below: An artist shows his paintings at an exhibition held at the Artisan Center in Damascus.

32

Left: **A Syrian man performs a dance at a restaurant popular with tourists.**

Music and Dance

Syrians express themselves through song and dance at family functions. Professional song and dance groups are often hired to help families celebrate at weddings and on other happy occasions. A popular traditional folk dance called *debke* (dib-KE) is often performed. Debke is sometimes danced by men only or women only and is similar to a group dance with dancers in a line.

Theater

Syrian theater is often used as a political instrument. The actors, playwrights, and directors are known for their radical views and their willingness to risk their freedom to get their messages across. Duraid Laham is one of Syria's most famous actors. He is known all over the Arab world as a comedy actor, but throughout the 1970s, his work focused more on politics. His popularity stems from his portrayal of victims of the Syrian political system. In recent years, Laham has also moved into directing.

A strong trend in Syrian theater since the 1990s has been for actors to take on the role of director. Actor/director Ghassan Masoud and actor/writer Talab Nasser are two who have filled this job. Syrian theater actors and actresses have also crossed over to other media. Television actress Karis Bashar starred in her first movie, *Sundook al Dunia* (Life Box), in 2002.

SYRIAN SINGERS

Two well-known Syrian singers are Asala Nasri and George Wassouf. Nasri has recorded many albums, and Wassouf is known throughout the Middle East. A newcomer to the Syrian music scene is Rowaida Attiyeh, who was the runner-up in a popular Middle-Eastern talent contest called "Superstar."

Leisure and Festivals

The population in Syria can be grouped into the "haves" and the "have-nots." Those who have money tend to live a modern lifestyle that includes holidays abroad. Those who are less well off often struggle just to make ends meet.

The majority of Syrians spend their leisure and festival time mainly with close friends and family, perhaps going on a picnic if weather permits or having a barbecue. Syrians love barbecues. Syrian barbecue grills, called *al manqal* (al-MAN-kal), are often made of a simple, rectangular aluminium box with holes at the base. Meat and vegetables are put on skewers or on a wire mesh and placed over the box containing charcoal, or *fahm* (FA-him). This inexpensive barbecue set can be bought at any hardware store for a few Syrian pounds. Often, Syrian families take their barbecues and some charcoal with them and pick a picturesque part of the countryside for their cookout.

HAMMAM — A SYRIAN TRADITION

The *hammam* (HAM-mum), or public bathhouse, has played an important role in Middle Eastern culture. Although there are fewer public hammams in the country today, Syrians still enjoy this tradition.
(A Closer Look, page 56)

Below: Syrian families often go on picnics as it is a fun and inexpensive activity that they can enjoy together.

Men spend their leisure time with friends at coffee houses, which are found in every village and city. Coffee houses offer two types of coffee. Traditional coffee is served very strong, without sugar, and spiced with cardamom. The other choice is Turkish coffee. This is also very strong and is served in tiny cups with lots of sugar added. Arabic tea is also sold in coffee shops. The tea is served in tiny glasses and is often flavored with mint and lots of sugar. Sweets and pastries are also available at coffee houses.

Coffee houses are not considered suitable places for women and are exclusively for men. Women meet in their homes for tea, coffee, and often homemade Syrian pastries and sweets. As in most traditional Arab societies, men and women do not socialize unless they are members of the same family.

Syrian children rarely have access to the computers, video games, and toys that children in other parts of the world might take for granted. Syrian children spend a large part of their day in school and completing their homework. During whatever free time they may have, Syrian children help their parents. Boys assist their fathers in the family business, while girls stay indoors and complete household chores with their mothers.

Above: Groups of men meet their friends for a drink and to talk at a teahouse in the old district of Tartus.

Below: One popular pastime with Syrian men is smoking a traditional water pipe.

Sports

As in much of the Middle East, the most popular sport in Syria is soccer. The top teams playing in the Syrian professional soccer league include Hutteen, Yakaza, Karama, and Wathba. Many people support their teams by attending matches at the stadiums. Others watch the matches that are shown on television for a few hours each week. Young children also love the game and often play soccer in the streets. Basketball is another popular sport in the country, and teams compete in a basketball league.

Since President Bashar al-Assad took office, he appears to be encouraging the development of sports as an activity for everyone. In 2003, the Syrian government entered into sports cooperation agreements with Lebanon and Croatia in an effort to advance Syria's sporting programs.

Syria has competed in many international sporting events and has hosted competitions such as the 1976 and 1992 Pan-Arab Games and the 1987 Mediterranean Games. At the 1996 Olympic games in Atlanta, Ghada Shouaa won the heptathlon, an athletic contest for women consisting of seven individual track-and-field events.

Above: **One of Syria's best-known athletes, Ghada Shouaa raises her arms in victory after winning the gold medal in the high jump at the 9th Pan-Arab Games competition in 1999.**

Left: **Syria's national soccer team, which played against the Philippines in May 2001 in Aleppo. The two nations were trying to qualify for the finals of the 2002 World Cup.**

Arabian Horses

Breeding and racing the famous Asil Arabian horses originated with the Bedouins of Syria and the surrounding countries. Despite their varying fortunes, this has remained a passionate interest through the years. To record the many families of Arab horses being bred in Syria, the Syrian government began publishing the Syrian Arab Horse Stud Book in July 1990. This document is accepted by the World Arabian Horse Organization (WAHO) and contains details on over one thousand purebred Arabian horses. The book, however, does not have a record of all Arabian horses in Syria. Many Bedouins living in rural areas did not want to register their animals, because the concept of the stud book was not properly explained to them. They were afraid that their horses might be seized by the goverment if they were to submit details of the animals for registration.

The Syrian registration committee is very careful about the horses that it registers, and not all horses submitted make it onto the register. The Syrian Ministry of Agriculture has now published the fifth volume of the Stud Book, which includes information about foals born up to 1999. There are now an estimated 1,200 Arabian horses and 247 owners and breeders, with about 260 broodmares and 95 stallions being bred.

Holidays and Festivals

Syria celebrates both religious and secular holidays. The first event on the Syrian calendar is New Year's Day, which is celebrated on January 1.

Revolution Day on March 8 marks the anniversary of the March 1963 revolution when the Baath Party assumed power in Syria. To commemorate the day, rallies are usually organized, and prominent leaders give speeches.

On May 6, 1915, members of the Al Fatat, an underground Arab group, were arrested for plotting against the government. Twenty-one members were publicly hung. May 6 is now remembered as Martyrs' Day. This event is also observed in neighboring Lebanon, because the two nations were once a single country and shared a common history until after World War I.

Independence Day on April 17 marks the day in 1946 when the French occupation of Syria ended. Other secular holidays observed in the country are Mother's Day on March 21 and Labor Day on May 1.

Easter is observed on two different dates. The first is celebrated by Catholic, Protestant, and Armenian Orthodox churches. The second date is recognized by the Syrian and Greek Orthodox churches. Syria's Christians celebrate Christmas, some on January 6, but it is a simpler occasion than in many other countries.

RAMADAN IN SYRIA

Ramadan is the ninth month of the Muslim calendar, during which all Muslims fast from sunrise to sunset. All over the Middle East, Muslims like to break their fasts during Ramadan with a selection of sweets.

(A Closer Look, page 68)

Left: **Islam forbids the depiction of people or animals, so decorations for religious holidays often feature just simple text or verses from the Quran. These flags celebrate the annual pilgrimage that Muslims make to the holy city of Mecca.**

Islamic Holidays

For Muslims, there are three main religious festivals every year. The most important holiday is Ramadan, which is a month of fasting. During this period, Muslims may not eat or drink from sunrise to sunset. Ramadan ends with a three-day feast called *Eid al-Fitr* (EED al-FIT-er). The feast begins with a prayer that takes place about an hour after dawn on the first day. Muslims dress in their finest clothes and visit friends and relatives. Even dead family members are remembered when close relatives visit the cemetery. Often, large families or organizations have one huge party or gathering to make it easier for everyone. Sweets are traditionally served to guests along with highly spiced coffee and tea served in tiny decorative cups.

The second most important festival for Muslims comes at the end of the *hajj* (HAJ) period and is called *Eid al-Adha* (EED al-AD-ha), or the Feast of the Sacrifice. At this time, those people who have not made the Hajj pilgrimage sacrifice a sheep or a cow. Afterward, the festivities are much the same as for the first Eid, with families and friends visiting one another.

The third important religious festival celebrated by Muslims in Syria is the Prophet Muhammad's birthday. The date for this event varies from year to year, depending on the lunar calendar.

Above: **All mosques, such as this one in Damascus, have a separate area for women to pray.**

Food

Syrian food is delicious, and Syrian cooks pride themselves on using top quality spices for cooking. These spices include cinnamon, cloves, and nutmeg. Perhaps the most notable aspect of Syrian food is the *mezze* (me-ZIH), which is an assortment of appetizers. The mezze consists of over forty little dishes that are served together with bread. They may include such delights as a chick pea paste called hummus, another type of paste made from tahini (sesame) paste and baked eggplant known as *baba ghanoush* (BA-ba ga-NOOJ), and many other little delicacies. Mezze is usually followed by a main dish of lamb, chicken, or fish. *Bulgar* (BUL-gah) is also eaten in Syria. Bulgar is made from wheat that has been boiled, dried, and crushed. The dry mixture is made into a dough and rolled into balls filled with meat, onions, and nuts.

Staples of the Syrian diet are bread, olive oil, and preserved dairy foods such as white cheese, similar to Greek feta cheese. Although Syrians eat a variety of breads, the most common is the flat, round loaf commonly known as pita bread in the West.

Below: **Preserved fruits and nuts are delicious eaten on their own or when used as an ingredient in dishes.**

Many types of fruits are grown in Syria, including grapefruit, oranges, pears, figs, apricots, olives, plums, and grapes. Some of these fruits are also preserved so that they can be enjoyed all year. Crystallized fruits, such as figs, pears, apples, and persimmons, are a Syrian delicacy. These are often sold in an assortment packed in wooden boxes.

Apricots are also used to make a paste that is sold in sheets and later made into an apricot drink called *qamareddine* (kumm-er-i-DEEN). The drink is made by tearing the sheets into small pieces and adding boiling water. Later, the resulting mixture is sweetened and cooled. Qamareddine is a fixture at every table during the Muslim holy month of Ramadan to help break the fast.

Syrian Meals

In Syria, people often help themselves from one large serving dish in the middle of the table. This is usually a meat and rice dish surrounded by side dishes, such as salad, yogurt, and other appetizers. If guests are present, the men and women separate. It is almost unheard of in traditional Syrian society for strange men and women to sit and eat together.

A CLOSER LOOK AT SYRIA

Although Syria only achieved independence in 1946, the country has a rich history dating back thousands of years. Syria has been home to many different civilizations. The Romans, Greeks, Arabs, and French are just some of the people who have lived in this land. Each group of people has left behind a rich legacy that includes architecture and buildings, arts and artifacts, language, and even their religion.

Today, Syria is a fascinating blend of old and new. Ancient ruins from Roman times, such as those at Bosra, contrast with the stunning Omayyad Mosque in Damascus from the seventh century

Opposite: **This young lady is dressed in traditional Bedouin attire. Bedouins are nomadic Arab tribes living in Syria.**

and the twelfth century remains of crusader castles, such as Crac des Chevaliers. Likewise, the simple yet charming water wheels of Hamah exist along with the technology of the Euphrates Dam.

The challenges facing Syria today are many. One of the most important is to improve and develop its economic policies so as to provide a decent standard of living for its people. In addition, the country needs to address the status of the Golan Heights, its relationship with Israel, and the number of troops it still has in neighboring Lebanon, where Syria has had a military presence since 1976.

Above: **Homs is the third most important city in Syria. The city sits on a hill 1,666 feet (508 m) above sea level and is located within a fertile agricultural region.**

Bosra

Bosra is one of Syria's most ancient and interesting cities. In addition to having one of the most well-preserved Roman amphitheaters in the world, Bosra was also the first Muslim city in Syria. It has the oldest surviving example of the square minarets that are common in Islamic architecture.

The most riveting part of the city today is the famous Roman theater, built in the second century A.D. This breathtakingly beautiful theater is a true architectural wonder in comparison to others built during the same time period in that it stands on its own instead of being built into the side of a hill. Another unusual feature is the fortress built around the theater, which has helped preserve it in excellent condition.

Bosra contains many other ruins dating to its inclusion in the Roman Empire, including baths, columns, and huge ornamental gates. There are also a few historically important mosques.

Much of Bosra is built from black basalt blocks, found in and around the town. Black basalt is actually solidified lava, and its great strength can resist erosion. Newer structures have

Below: **During its prime, the Roman amphitheater at Bosra could seat fifteen thousand spectators.**

Above: **The design of this cathedral at Bosra includes many arches.**

often been erected over and around ancient Roman buildings. Bosra was once at the crossroads of major trade routes and was a stopover for Muslims making a pilgrimage to Mecca. Today, all of Bosra is a potential archeological dig site. In many places, pavements and roads have been dug up in order to try to find ancient thoroughfares. Bosra was designated a UNESCO world heritage site in 1980. Preservation efforts are underway to protect the remaining archways, minarets, and stately buildings that made Bosra beautiful. This is also probably why there is a government program to relocate the few residents living in the ancient city to a newer community outside the city walls.

Bosra was mentioned in documents left by the Egyptian pharaohs and is even referred to in the Bible. A key city in the first century, it was conquered by the Romans and became their regional capital in A.D. 106.

After the fall of the Roman empire, Bosra continued to grow as it had links with both early Christianity and Islam. A Christian archbishop was based there, and it is believed that the Prophet Muhammad visited the city when he was a boy. Afterward, a monk named Bahira predicted Muhammad's role as the founder of Islam.

Crac des Chevaliers

The crusader castles were built as defensive retreats for use by the Knights Hospitallers during the Crusades. Crac des Chevaliers has been described as perhaps the most stunning and well preserved of all the crusader castles in Europe and the former Ottoman Empire.

Built in the twelfth century, Crac des Chevaliers covers an area of 7.4 acres (3 hectares). It has thirteen towers and a network of stores, tanks, corridors, and bridges. The castle could accommodate two thousand soldiers, five hundred horses, equipment, and enough supplies for five years.

Known principally by its Arabic name of Qalaat Al Hosn, or the Castle of the Knights, the fortress is situated on what was historically an important defensive site, a gap in the mountain range between the city of Homs and the Mediterranean.

Crac des Chevaliers is famous throughout the Middle East, and many visitors come to Syria just to visit it. Perhaps the main reason this fortress holds such fascination for so many

THE CRUSADES

From the late eleventh century to the late thirteenth century, the Christians living in Europe launched a series of wars, called crusades, to try and recover former Christian lands that had fallen under Muslim rule.

Below: Crac des Chevaliers was constructed from locally hewn basalt stone. Additions of limestone can be distinguished from the original structure.

Left: Although slightly worn down today, the beautiful vaulted ceiling in the castle's great chamber gives visitors an idea of how magnificent the space must have been when it was occupied.

people is simply because of its combination of good design, beauty, romance, history, and location. No other remaining crusader castle so well represents the age of the Crusades when European knights struggled to wrest the Holy Lands from the Muslims who occupied them.

Although Crac des Chevaliers is considerably well preserved, it still has a certain amount of decay. Since 1934, restoration work has been carried out on the fortress, and it is undoubtedly this work that should be credited for the condition of the castle today.

While Crac des Chevalier proved an excellent fortification and remained impregnable throughout much of the Crusades, it did eventually fall. In 1271, the Muslims triumphed over the crusaders when Mameluk Sultan Beybars finally recovered the castle after a long siege.

Damascus

Located in southwestern Syria, Damascus sits on a terrace 2,250 feet (685 m) above sea level on the edge of the Anti-Lebanon Mountains. The city overlooks the fertile floodplain of the Barada River, which also flows through the city. As the capital of Syria, Damascus is the center of government. It is also the country's largest city, with a population of about 2.2 million people, and it is the center of business and commerce.

It is thought that Damascus may be the oldest continuously inhabited city in the world. New archaeological finds indicate that the city was first inhabited in 8000 B.C. Nothing much is known, however, about its earliest people.

Left: **A view over the modern city of Damascus, which is also called** *Dimashq* **in Arabic.**

Damascus has always been a thriving and economically influential city. It was fought over and conquered by many countries and leaders, including Nebuchadnezzar and Alexander the Great. Over the centuries, the city has been ruled by the Arameans, the Assyrians, the Greeks, the Persians, the Romans, the Byzantines, the Omayyads, the Ottomans, and the French.

Not surprisingly, Damascus today has many ancient and modern landmarks that reflect the many years and people who have inhabited it throughout history.

The city is of importance in Christian history as it was on the road to Damascus where Saul of Tarsus had a vision that led to his conversion to Christianity. He became St. Paul the Apostle.

In A.D. 635, Damascus became part of the Islamic Omayyad Empire and was its capital from A.D. 661 to 750. The magnificent Omayyad Mosque was built during this period.

Between 1516 and 1918, Damascus was part of the Turkish Ottoman Empire. Eventually Arabs joined with the British and French in efforts to break up this Islamic empire. The Ottoman Empire fell, and eventually Damascus and the rest of the surrounding area came under the control of Britain or France at the end of World War I.

Above: **Souks are the traditional equivalent of a shopping mall. Souk Al-Hamidiyyah is an ancient market that has existed on the same site in the Old City of Damascus for hundreds of years.**

Dead Cities of Aleppo

Aleppo, the second largest city in Syria, is surrounded by a cluster of ruins and historical sites that are known as the Dead Cities. These Dead Cities date back to late-Roman and Byzantine times and are the well-preserved remains of about seven hundred villages that flourished in the fourth century A.D., toward the end of the Roman Empire. Set about 2 to 3 miles (3 to 5 km) apart, the villages feature buildings made from a local grey stone. It is only their distinctive architecture that hints of their history.

Although the ruins attracted attention in the late nineteenth century and were again the subject of interest in the 1930s, it was not until the 1970s that intensive study began. Georges Tate and Jean-Pierre Sodini of the French Institute of Archaeology in Damascus excavated the village of Dehes and found evidence that the villagers raised livestock and grew crops. Their research also indicates a continuous period of expansion from the end of the third century until about A.D. 550. By then, the area had an estimated population of about 300,000.

Below: **The ruins of this citadel at Aleppo date back to the thirteenth century and are an excellent example of Arab military architecture.**

Left: **The ruins of this church, built in honor of St. Simeon Stylites, feature a series of arches, which are an architectural feature used during the rule of the Roman Empire.**

The Dead Cities slowly declined as a result of invasions, illness, and natural disasters. From the eighth century on, the area was gradually abandoned.

Among the best known of the Dead Cities is Qalaat Semaan, northwest of Aleppo. It was named after St. Simeon Stylites, a fifth century monk who lived as a hermit on the top of a rock pillar for thirty-eight years. Initially, he was only about 10 feet (3 m) off the ground, but as more and more people learned of him and sought his advice, he was constantly disturbed. So he added to his pillar several times. In the end, it is said he was perched about 65 feet (20 m) off the ground. According to historical archives, St. Simeon Stylites would preach twice a day and offer spiritual advice to those who visited him. After his death in A.D. 459, the largest church at that time was built in his honor.

Southwest of Aleppo is Ebla, another site with a rich history dating to 2600 B.C. In the 1970s, Ebla was the focus of attention in the archaeological world when seventeen thousand clay tablets were discovered there that revealed the first alphabet in Sumerian cuneiform writing and signs of ancient international commerce.

Euphrates Dam

In 1968, construction started on the Euphrates Dam, which became one of the largest earth-filled dams in the world. Located 30 miles (50 km) from a town called Ar-Raqqah in north-central Syria, the dam, also known as the Thawra "Revolution" Dam or the Tabaqah Dam, is the country's pride and joy.

The dam is filled with approximately 1,447 million cubic feet (41 million cubic meters) of earth, rock, and clay and is reinforced by concrete walls that are approximately 197 feet (60 m) high and 2.8 miles (4.5 km) long. The dam is 1,680 feet (512 m) wide at the bottom, decreasing to 62 feet (19 m) at the top.

When the dam was completed in 1973, a reservoir formed behind it. Named Lake Al-Assad, the reservoir provides the area with a vital irrigation source. The lake is about 50 miles (80 km) long and averages about 5 miles (8 km) wide. By 1999, the Euphrates Dam had been instrumental in salvaging about 1.59 million acres (644,000 hectares) of agricultural land in Syria. Although the water situation is vastly improved, the dam has not led to the agricultural output that was hoped for as a result of improved irrigation.

Below: **Construction of the Euphrates Dam has provided agricultural areas with irrigation and opened up more areas for farming. Here, neat fields of crops grow along the banks of the Euphrates.**

The power plant that services the dam was finally completed in 1977. The hydroelectric station can generate one million kilowatts of power when the water passes through the dam and rotates its turbines. The power output fluctuates because of the fluctuating water level of the dam. As a result, some regions of Syria suffered many cuts in power during the 1980s and early 1990s until steps were taken to keep the power output constant.

In 2001, the Turkish government unveiled plans to build a network of dams along the Euphrates in Turkey that may further reduce the effectiveness of the Syrian Dam project. Syria and Iraq oppose Turkey's plans because they estimate that the flow of water to their two countries will be further reduced. During the early-to-mid 1990s, Turkey reduced the flow of the Euphrates into Syria to such an extent that seven of the ten dam turbines had to be halted. When the Syrian dam was completed, the flow of the Euphrates into Iraq was also drastically reduced. This almost led to a war between the two nations in 1974 when Iraq threatened to bomb the dam and both sides deployed troops to the border. Fortunately, diplomats from the Soviet Union and Saudi Arabia resolved the dispute peaceably.

Above: **The control tower of the Euphrates Dam manages all the operations of the dam and controls the supply of water to its hydroelectric station.**

Golan Heights

The Golan Heights gets its name from a city called "Golan in Bashan" that is mentioned in the Bible. This narrow strip of Syrian land that marks the border with Israel also shares a border with south Lebanon and northwest Jordan. Because of its strategic location, it has been an area of controversy in the Middle East for decades.

The area is beautiful, and some of the most precious plants and animals in the Middle East inhabit the Golan. Mount Hermon is in the north. The plateau was once actively volcanic, and the northernmost points remain weathered and desolate.

On June 5, 1967, the Six-Day War started. Fighting broke out between Israel and Syria, and by June 10, Israeli troops had captured the area between the two countries, which totals 444 square miles (1,150 sq km). The Golan, the Israelis say, represents a necessary defense against possible Syrian attack because of its high elevation. The Syrians, on the other hand, value this piece of land for its abundance of water and refuse to relinquish their claim to it.

Former Syrian President Hafez al-Assad tried hard to get back the Golan Heights, and in 1973, there was another war, the Yom Kippur War, over the dispute. In 1967, over 100,000 Arabs

Left: **French-built Israeli tanks in action in June 1967. The Israelis captured the Golan Heights in 1967 and annexed the area in 1981. Since then, the two nations have held peace talks but have not successfully negotiated a final agreement over this land.**

living there fled the fighting, 80,000 going to Syria and 20,000 to Lebanon. These refugees have not been allowed to return for various political reasons, and by the late 1970s, the Israelis had set up nearly thirty Jewish settlements in the area, firming up their claim to sovereignty.

Above: **The southern portion of the Golan Heights boasts some of the most fertile land in the area.**

In 1975, after lengthy mediation by the Unites States, the Israelis gave back a small amount of land in Al-Qunaytirah province. By 1981, the Golan was officially annexed by Israel's government. This annexation was not recognized internationally. The Golan, however, remains under Israeli occupation.

Since the peace process began in 1991, Israel and Syria have not stopped arguing over the Golan. In December 1999, Israeli-Syrian talks resumed after a nearly four-year break. From Syria's point of view, normalization of relations between the two countries largely depended on Israel agreeing to withdraw from the Golan Heights. From Israel's point of view, giving up the Golan Heights, which has served as a buffer zone between the two nations, could not occur without a guarantee of Israel's national security. By January 2000, however, talks broke down when Syria demanded a detailed discussion on the return of the entire Golan Heights. What will happen next in the dispute is not certain.

Hammam – A Syrian Tradition

For centuries, hammams, or public bathhouses, have played an important role in Middle Eastern culture. The tradition of public baths in Syria and the surrounding area was probably started by the Greeks and then carried on by the Romans as both of these cultures expanded their empires to Syria. The traditions that started in ancient times have continued because cleanliness is an important aspect of Islamic life. Until modern times, public baths have always been a practical way for the poor to stay clean.

After the fall of Constantinople in 1453, the Roman bath was adopted and adapted to Muslim preferences by the Muslim Ottoman conquerors. Ritual bathing and cleanliness are intrinsic to Islam. The Islamic bath is a combination of the religious bathing tradition of the Muslims and the elaborate bathing rituals

Left: **The locker room of a hammam. The attendant sits at a table in the center of the room and issues towels to bathers. The hooks on the wall are for hanging one's clothes.**

of the Romans. Throughout much of Syria and the surrounding areas, these public baths were established in close proximity to mosques as a facility for praying.

Hammams in Syria are strictly segregated. Public baths for women are a comparative rarity, because it is not considered proper for Muslim women to take off their clothes in any public place with strangers.

The kind of public baths found in Syria are called Turkish baths in the West, and this is a good indication that many of Syria's hammams began with the Ottoman Empire. A Turkish bath has a room where bathers are subjected to hot, dry air that makes them sweat profusely. They then plunge into cold water and often repeat the process, with intermediate sessions of vigorous massage.

Although old public hammams have declined in recent years, there are still a number of them in Syria. In Damascus, the 800-year-old an-Nureddin is among the most famous and popular public bath. Others in the city include Hammam al-Ward and Hammam al-Malek al-Dhaher.

Above: **The hammams in Syria are lavishly decorated with mosaic designs in the Roman tradition and often include fountains and decorative pools.**

An Influential Leader

Khalid Ibn al-Walid was a leader of the expanded Muslim empire in its early days. Although he battled against the Prophet Muhammad at Ohud in A.D. 625, Khalid later converted to Islam and joined forces with Muhammad in the conquest of Mecca. Afterward, the Prophet gave him the title "Sword of Allah," and he led a number of missions to and conquests of provinces that were in the process of abandoning Islamic beliefs. Khalid's fighting was so intense that he is known for breaking nine swords during the Battle of Mutah, in what is now southern Jordan. Due to his superior military skills, there were only twelve Muslim casualties against the combined forces of the Roman and Arab armies.

The second caliph of Islam, Umar Ibn al-Khattab, extended Islam's rule over Egypt, Syria, Iraq, and Persia. Within four years after the death of the Prophet, the Muslim state had extended its influence over all of Syria with the commander-in-chief of the Muslim army, Khalid Ibn al-Walid, at their head.

Left: **The main features of the Khalid Ibn Al-Walid Mosque in the city of Homs are a pair of tall stone minarets and the enormous metal domes.**

The Muslims administered the new territories with tolerance toward non-Muslims. At Damascus, for example, after taking the city following a six-month siege, Khalid Ibn al-Walid signed a treaty that read as follows: "The inhabitants of greater Syria are promised security for their lives, property and churches. Their city wall shall not be demolished, neither shall any Muslim be quartered in their houses. Thereunto we give them the pact of Allah and the protection of His Prophet, the caliphs and the believers. So long as they pay the poll tax."

After signing the Damascus treaty, Khalid was asked by Caliph Umar to step down as commander of the army. Khalid continued to lend his military knowledge to the new commander-in-chief and continued to live in Syria. The last seven years of his life were spent in the city of Homs, and he died in A.D. 641 at the age of fifty-five. In 1908, the Ottomans built an imposing mosque in his honor. Today, the Khalid Ibn Al-Walid Mosque is a main attraction and one of the most significant historic buildings in the city of Homs, but this architectural monument says little of the man himself.

Above: **A staunch Muslim, Khalid did not allow any sketches or images of himself to be made. The Khalid Ibn Al-Walid Mosque was built to honor and remember him, and its beautiful and grand interior reflects the greatness of the man.**

Maalula

Thirty-one miles (50 km) north of Damascus is the old-fashioned village of Maalula. Perched high on the eastern slope of the Anti-Lebanon range, this picturesque rural community sits at an altitude of more than 4,920 feet (1,500 m).

Many of the houses in the village are painted blue, yellow, or purple and are built into the face of a large cliff. The charming buildings make a striking contrast against the greenery of trees and shrubs that grow on the mountain slopes.

Maalula is filled with history, and despite its tiny population of only 2,000, the village has an atmosphere of a much larger community. Maalula is famous because its residents still speak Aramaic, the language spoken by Jesus Christ. This almost-extinct

Left: **From a distance, the village of Maalula looks like stacks of little cubes built into the mountain.**

Above: **The Convent of St. Tekla includes a series of open terraces as well as a modern church with a striking silver dome.**

language is only spoken in Maalula and two neighboring villages. Maalula's remote location and harsh climate may have helped to preserve the language.

The ancestors of the Maalula residents were the Semitic tribes who lived in the Syrian Desert many hundreds of years ago. According to ancient manuscripts, these tribes were called Aramu or Ahlamu, and their main spoken language was Aramaic. Later, the area fell to the Assyrians and became part of the Assyrian Empire from about 840 B.C. to 609 B.C. Aramaic was spoken throughout the Assyrian Empire. In the seventh century A.D., Islam spread throughout the entire region, and Arabic became the major language, displacing all others. Afterward, the use of Aramaic declined rapidly.

One famous landmark in Maalula is the Catholic monastery of St. Sergius built in the fourth century. The compound also includes a church and tombs dating back to the Byzantine period. Another landmark is the orthodox Convent of St. Tekla, named for a native of Turkey. Tekla converted to Christianity and left her family in order to devote her life to God.

Norias of Hamah

Many hundreds of years ago, a collection of *norias* (NO-rias), or wooden water wheels, were built in and around the city of Hamah (also known as Hama) to supply water to the city for daily use and irrigation. Only seventeen norias still stand today. Although they are operational, these gigantic wooden water wheels are now more of a tourist attraction for Hamah, a town sandwiched between Homs and Aleppo on the banks of the Orontes River.

A noria operates by means of the water passing beneath it. With this ancient technique, the wheel raises water from a pool or a well to a channel or a container above. Unlike a water mill, the wheel does not run any machinery. Instead, the wheel has wooden boxes mounted around its rim that scoop water from the river and carry it to the top, where it falls into a trough alongside the wheel. The water then flows through aqueducts and pipes to irrigate farm fields or to provide domestic water supplies. The amount of water generated by the noria is small compared to modern hydraulic plants, but because it is being powered by the flow of the river itself, the noria costs nothing to operate and lasts for a very long time.

The wheels of Hamah's norias range between 33 and 66 feet (10 and 20 m) in diameter. The largest remaining noria is called al-Muhammadiyah, and until 1981, it still supplied the Grand Mosque with water. Much of the old town, including this mosque, was destroyed during internal troubles in 1982, when as many as 20,000 civilians were massacred by government forces in one month. Some buildings have survived, and many others, including the Grand Mosque, are being reconstructed.

Other norias in Hamah include those in the town center, located in the middle of a beautiful public park. Another popular place with visitors is the Four Norias of Bishriatt on the eastern side of Hamah, about one-half mile (1 km) upriver from the town center.

The norias of Hamah produce a distinctive sound that is created by the friction between the wooden wheel and the blocks they are mounted on. The sound has been likened to a human cry or the creaking of a cart. This unique sound can be heard throughout the town.

Above: Detail of a noria. Today, water from the Orontes River is still used to water gardens in Hamah.

Opposite: Although many norias are still operational today, most of them serve a decorative function and are more of a tourist attraction than an actual means of drawing water from the river.

Omayyad Mosque

The Omayyad Mosque, which sits in the center of the Old City of Damascus, is one of the gems of Islamic architecture and is considered the fourth holiest Islamic site. This glorious structure was built by the Omayyad Caliph al-Walid ibn Abdul Malek in A.D. 705 when Damascus was the heart of the Arab Islamic empire.

Situated at the east end of Souq al-Hamidiyyah, the Omayyad Mosque was converted from an earlier Christian cathedral dedicated to John the Baptist. This church was built by the Roman Emperor Theodosius on a site once used for pagan sacrifices in honor of the Roman god Jupiter.

Although the Arabs conquered the city in A.D. 635, Muslims and Christians agreed to share the building's space. The Muslims added a structure against the southern wall, and the two religions worshipped side by side. Over time, the number of Christians in Damascus dwindled, and the number of Muslims grew. The

Below: **The Omayyad Mosque boasts an enormous courtyard, which contains the Dome of the Hours, the Dome of the Treasure, and the ablutions fountain.**

Left: **The interior of the Omayyad Mosque, showing the Shrine of John the Baptist. The walls of the mosque are covered in marble and mosaic panels.**

caliph struck a deal with the Christians to give up their part of the building in exchange for the construction of a new church as well as several plots of land to build more churches.

Renovation and construction of the mosque took place over a period of ten years and cost eleven million gold dinars. The finest architects from Constantinople, Egypt, and Damascus worked on the Omayyad Mosque, and it is one of only a few mosques in the Muslim world that has three minarets. The Omayyad Mosque became the prototype for hundreds of mosques around the world.

For travelers, the grandeur and peace of the Omayyad Mosque is a welcome relief from the heat and noise outside. Non-Muslims are welcome to visit, but visitors must put on the black robes provided before entering the mosque.

Queen of Palmyra

Queen Zenobia, who claimed to be a direct descendant of Cleopatra, reigned over the desert city of Palmyra from A.D. 267 to 272. She was a woman ahead of her time. Queen Zenobia was admired for her beauty and style, her strong character, and her courage.

According to historians, Queen Zenobia loved to dress in purple, which was a color reserved for royalty and nobility. She spoke Greek, Latin, Egyptian, Aramaic, and Arabic and was well-versed in politics. She even wrote a book on Oriental history. A skilled horsewoman, Queen Zenobia regularly rode with her soldiers, wearing her purple robes, her head shielded by a helmet.

Historians have given the impression that Zenobia was responsible for Palmyra's great glory. It was her husband, Septimius Odenathus, however, who had raised Palmyra to its height by skillful diplomacy with the Romans and his military skills. Zenobia, with her unchecked ambition, was eventually responsible for Palmyra's downfall.

After the death of Odenathus and his eldest son, Zenobia took the throne as regent for her young son. She had some military success and expanded Palmyra's borders by conquering Syria, Egypt, and Anatolia, now part of Turkey. Unfortunately, Queen Zenobia had even greater ambitions. She broke off all the political ties that her husband had so carefully made with Rome and declared Palmyra's complete independence. Her image began to appear beside that of her son, Wahballat, on coins, milestones, and papyrus or parchment documents, in open defiance of Rome.

The Roman Emperor Aurelian could not allow such insubordination and sent his troops to fight her. Queen Zenobia's rule came to an abrupt end when she was defeated in battle by the Romans in A.D. 272. Queen Zenobia still refused to surrender. Rather than accept defeat, some say that she poisoned herself. Other accounts state that Zenobia was captured and paraded through the streets of Rome in chains of pure gold, or that she was banished by Aurelian and died living in exile outside Rome.

Afterwards, the prosperity of Palmyra ended. Ravaged by several natural and man-made disasters over the next centuries, Palmyra slipped quietly into history.

Above: **The ancient city of Palmyra contains some of Syria's most important ruins. These columns once formed part of the agora, which is the equivalent of a market place.**

Opposite: **Considered the most noble and beautiful woman of her time, Queen Zenobia had a tan complexion, black eyes, and pearly white teeth.**

Ramadan in Syria

Ramadan is the ninth month of the Muslim year, during which all healthy Muslim adolescents and adults practice *sawm* (SOWM), or fasting from sunrise to sundown. Fasting means that they eat or drink nothing. Ramadan is based on a lunar calendar, which is eleven days shorter, so the date of the event varies from year to year.

In Syria, Ramadan is welcomed with cannon fire during the early part of the night, a signal that the new moon has been seen. This sighting is a necessary condition before proclaiming the start of Ramadan and is the reason that Muslim communities in different parts of the world may start Ramadan on different days.

As the sun sets each day, the call to prayer is heard, and Muslim families gather to break their fast with a meal called *iftar* (if-TAR) that usually begins with dates and a drink of water. After this course, some people pray the fourth prayer of the day, *maghrib* (magh-RIB), or the dusk prayer, while others complete their meal before praying.

Below: **Ramadan is a time for reflection. During this month, Muslims visit the mosque and spend time praying and studying the Quran.**

Left: **During the month of Ramadan, most people try to help the poor and needy by providing food and other aid. Some people may even donate a whole sheep or goat to orphanages and other charity organizations.**

When the call for the night prayer, *isha* (i-SHA), rings out, men make their way to the mosques to pray the evening prayer followed by a special prayer for Ramadan called *tarawih* (ta-ra-WEEH). Women may pray at a mosque or at home. Almost all mosques have a section for women to pray in.

About an hour before dawn, most people eat a light meal called *sahur* (sa-HER) before the call for the dawn prayer, *Fajr* (FAJ), and the signal to start fasting again. Everyone tries to devote their time to good works. During Ramadan, they also try to read as much as they can of the Muslim holy book, the Quran. Most try to complete it at least once, although some people may manage to read it a few times. Life goes on as usual, although the time of events may be modified slightly to allow everyone to get home in time for the breaking of their fast.

Ramadan lasts until the new moon is sighted again, usually twenty-nine or thirty days later. The cannons sound once more to announce the end of Ramadan and the beginning of the three-day feast called *Eid al-Fitr*, or the Festival of Breaking the Fast.

Syrian Nature Reserves

In 1991, the first wildlife reserve in Syria, the Talila Reserve, was established in Homs province near Palmyra. One reason it was created was to protect the country's gazelles, which were close to becoming extinct.

As in much of the rest of the world, and especially this area of the Middle East, Syria's plants and animals have dwindled considerably during the past half century. Lack of attention to the needs of the environment and endangered species have led to this problem. Hunting is a national pastime for Arabs, and ignorance of the precarious situation of many species meant that no restrictions were put in place until 1994.

Following the publication of the Global Biodiversity Assessment by the United Nations Environmental Program in 1995, nature and wildlife reserves were established in the Middle East. One such nature reserve in Syria is Al Thawra Reserve on the island of the same name. Al Thawra Island was created upon the completion of the Euphrates Dam. After the dam was built, the water level slowly rose to form Lake Al-Assad. Areas of higher elevation formed several islands, one of which was Al Thawra.

The island is small, measuring just 1.24 miles (2 km) in length and 32 feet (10 m) in width, but Al Thawra is one example where man's interference in nature has actually had a positive effect on conservation. Al Thawra Island is one of four wildlife sanctuaries in Syria with a separate area for gazelles. The reserve is home to over 130 gazelles. As is true of some other desert animals, gazelles can survive without water for long periods of time. What is amazing, however, is that some gazelles do not even drink water. Instead, moisture in the foods they eat provides them with the fluids that they need. Wardens at the reserve expect to release the gazelles in a couple of years. As a first step, they intend to observe the behavior of six pairs of gazelles that are being put on another island. The Al Thawra Reserve is also home to plants, such as the olea and eucalyptus, and a number of bird species, such as the lesser kestrel and the see-see partridge.

Besides Talila Reserve and Al Thawra Reserve, the two other wildlife reserves that have been established in Syria are the Abdel-Aziz Mountain Reserve and the Al-Adama Reserve.

Opposite: **Pine trees are just one of the many species of trees that grow in abundance at the Al Thawra Nature Reserve.**

Below: **In addition to endangered species, common animals such as squirrels also make their home in the nature reserves.**

70

Ugarit

The ancient city of Ugarit lies 6 miles (10 km) north of Latakia on the Mediterranean coast. Records from Egyptian times contain the name of the city. Its location and other details about the city, however, remained a secret until 1928, when a female peasant plowing a field accidentally opened an ancient tomb. In 1929, French archaeologist Claude F. A. Schaeffer began digging at the site.

Early on in the excavation process, several clay tablets inscribed with cuneiform writing were found. These were discovered to be from libraries in a royal palace, a temple, and the homes of leading citizens. Some of the tablets were written in the ancient Babylonian language, but most of them were in a previously unknown language with thirty symbols. This language was named Ugaritic after the site.

Many notable archaeological discoveries have been made at Ugarit, with one of the most important finds being tablets from the fourteenth century B.C. The tablets were carved in Ugaritic. After deciphering these early alphabets, archaeologists

Below: **These ruins are of a fort dating back to 1400 B.C., which was once part of the ancient city of Ugarit.**

Left: **This Bronze Age clay tablet was discovered by archaeologists at Ugarit.**

reported that the tablets contain poems and myths of the ancient people of Canaan. The tablets prove that the stories of the Old Testament were based on Canaanite documents and were passed on by word of mouth.

In 1958, archaeologists discovered another library of tablets. Named the Claremont Ras Shamra Tablets, these were quickly sold on the black market and were not recovered until 1970.

The Ugarit tablets are of particular importance to scholars studying the Old Testament, because they echo some of what is contained in the Bible. The deciphering of the tablets has helped scholars to understand the meaning of passages in the Old Testament and the meaning of difficult old Hebrew words.

Subsequent excavations at the Ugarit site in 1994 turned up an additional 325 clay tablets. These were still awaiting cleaning and deciphering in 2003, as years of being underground have covered them in a thick layer of calcite that has rendered them illegible. It will be exciting to see what these tablets reveal.

RELATIONS WITH NORTH AMERICA

Although some of Syria's neighbors have excellent relations with North America, Syria has not enjoyed a relationship of cordiality and mutual cooperation with the United States. Syria's relations with the United States have mainly been troubled, from the U.S. perspective, by Syria's refusal to sign a peace treaty with Israel, and, from the Syrian perspective, by the steadfast support of the United States for Israel. This conflict has resulted in the United States imposing sanctions on Syria and halting all U.S. aid to Syria since the early 1980s.

Opposite: **Soldiers search for landmines during an exercise on the Golan Heights. Israel captured the area from Syria in 1967 and annexed it in 1981. The United States has tried to broker a peace agreement between Syria and Israel.**

In contrast, Canada enjoys a better relationship with Syria. The two countries have a long history of ties that go back to the late nineteenth century. Canadian Prime Minister Jean Chrétien has even made an official visit to Syria. In recent years, government officials and businessmen from both countries have visited each other to explore the opportunities of working together. The two countries have also collaborated in the areas of arts and education. Canada has hosted Syrian art exhibitions, and Canadian Resource Education Centers have been set up at universities in Syria.

Above: **President Hafez al-Assad of Syria (*left*) meets with President Bill Clinton of the United States (*right*) on March 26, 2000, in Geneva. President Clinton was trying to convince the Syrian president to make peace with Israel.**

U.S. Policy on Syria

The United States was not directly involved in the partitioning of the former Ottoman Empire, from which modern Syria was formed. The difficulties in the relations of the United States and Syria have been largely a result of Syria's past alliance with the Soviet Union, a major enemy of the United States before 1991, and its continuing hostility to Israel, an important U.S. ally.

Syria opposed the creation of the nation of Israel. Shortly after Israel declared its independence in 1948, Syria was among the nations surrounding Israel that attacked it without provocation. Following Syria's defeat by Israel, Syria entered a long period of political instability, lasting from about the late 1940s until about 1970. This period was marked by numerous coups and a short-lived union with Egypt. During this unstable time, the Syrian Communist Party and the Baath Party grew in power in Syria.

During the 1950s, in particular, Syria made a number of political moves that put it at odds with the United States. After elections on September 10, 1954, a government came to power in Syria that began building relations with the Soviet Union. Between 1954 and 1955, Turkey, Pakistan, Iraq, and Britain — with the support of the United States — signed a series of treaties known as the Baghdad Pact to counter the threat from the Soviet Union. Syria refused to join the pact. Instead, on August 6, 1957, Syria signed a treaty with the Soviet Union. Less than a week later, relations between Syria and the United States broke down completely, with Syria expelling three U.S. diplomats that it claimed were involved in a failed coup attempt and the United States asking Syria's ambassador to leave the country.

Syria's difficulties continued in the 1960s and 1970s. Although a 1961 coup broke Syria's brief union with Egypt, and the United States recognized Syria's new president, Nathim al-Qudsi, more coups made the Baath Party the dominant political party in Syria. In 1967, Syria lost the Golan Heights to Israel in the Six-Day War. Another war with Israel in 1973 also ended in Syria's defeat.

For much of the time that President Hafez al-Assad was in power, Syria was isolated from both the West and its Arab neighbors, mostly because of Assad's alliance with the Soviet Union. In the 1991 Gulf War, however, Syria did contribute about 20,000 troops to the coalition that drove Iraq out of Kuwait.

Left: **Syrian Foreign Minister Faruq al-Shara greets U.S. secretary of state Madeleine Albright upon her arrival in Damascus on September 4, 1999. The aim of Albright's visit was to persuade Syria to resume peace talks with Israel.**

The Question of Peace

The United States has been attempting to bridge differences between Syria and Israel for decades. The greatest stumbling blocks to an agreement are Israel's occupation of the Golan Heights, which has continued since 1967, and Syria's refusal to recognize Israel's right to exist. Syria has also been named as a country that promotes international terrorism.

In 1983, Syria rejected the Camp David Accords, the agreements in which Israel and Egypt made peace. In view of this rejection and Syria's continued alliance with the Soviet Union, the United States prohibited any aid to Syria. In the late 1990s, U.S. president Bill Clinton tried to mediate a Middle East peace agreement. Syria, however, refuses to make peace with Israel until all of the occupied territory of the Golan Heights is returned. Israel considers control of this territory to be essential to its security and is unwilling to return it. In October 2003, Israel bombed what it claimed were terrorist training camps in Syria.

At the end of December 2003, U.S.-Syrian relations were as tense as ever, after the United States accused Syria of harboring fugitives from the war in Iraq. Syria denies this accusation.

Right: **President Bill Clinton (***center***) of the United States, Israeli prime minister Ehud Barak (***right***), and Syrian foreign minister Faruq al-Shara (***left***) walk through the Rose Garden at the White House in December 1999. The foreign leaders were there at the invitation of President Clinton to discuss the possibility of peace between Syria and Israel.**

Left: **President Bashar al-Assad of Syria meets with the new U.S. ambassador to Syria, Margaret Scobey, on January 10, 2004. It is hoped that relations will improve with her appointment.**

Left: Syria's oil minister Maher Jamal (*center*) visits an oil fair organized in Damascus in 2000 by the oil ministry and international oil companies. Some of the international aid received by Syria has been used to develop its petroleum industry. Petroleum refining and the manufacture of petroleum products is an important industry in Syria.

Economic Aid to Syria

The United States has given Syria U.S. $627.5 million in aid since 1950. U.S. $34 million has been given for development assistance, U.S. $438 million for economic support, U.S. $155.4 million for food aid, and U.S. $61,000 for military training. Most of this aid was provided during a thaw in relations between the two countries from 1974 to 1979. Since 1981, Syria has not received any aid from the United States. Between 2000 and 2002, Syria received around U.S. $394 million in economic aid from other sources, including Canada. In talks involving the United States, Syria, and Israel, the United States has said that economic aid to Syria will not resume until Syria makes peace with Israel.

On December 18, 2003, the U.S. Congress passed the Syrian Accountability Act, which would impose additional U.S. sanctions against Syria unless it complied with conditions to counter international terrorism and ended its occupation of Lebanese territory. Under the act, Syria also had to stop producing weapons of mass destruction and importing illegal goods from Iraq, against whom U.S. sanctions were also in force.

EXEMPT FROM THE EMBARGO

Despite the tension between the United States and Syria, there is still some contact between the countries. For example, groups of Syrian government and professional representatives visit the United States on orientation tours that are part of the International Visitor Program. This program is run by the U.S. Information Agency, which is funded by the Department of State.

Syrian Emigration to the United States

In 1903, Syrian immigration to the United States began in earnest. That year alone, 5,551 Syrians came and settled. The next wave of Syrian emigration to the United States was in the late 1940s when about 10,000 Syrian Jews fled the country following the 1948 formation of the State of Israel.

Based on statistics from the 2000 population census, California, New York, Pennsylvania, and New Jersey were the states with the highest number of Americans of Syrian origin.

In the early twenty-first century, the United States tightened its immigration policies following the September 11, 2001 terrorist attacks. Syria has been affected because it is believed to be a country that has promoted terrorism.

U.S.-Syrian Trade

Since 1979, the United States has placed export trade restrictions on Syria. Today, thirty-three categories of products, including aircraft, vehicles, computers, and other high-technology goods, require a license for export to Syria. In 2002, the United States imported U.S. $148.07 million in Syrian goods, such as mineral oils, fuels, and antiques. Syria imported U.S. $274.05 million in U.S.-made goods such as food, machinery, and electrical appliances.

Left: Although wheat is grown in Syria, the yield is not enough to feed its people, so the country imports food from other nations. Although the United States has imposed restrictions on trade with Syria, food and medicine are not included under these restrictions.

Canadian-Syrian Relations

Canadian-Syrian relations go back over one hundred years and have always been considerably warmer than those between Syria and the United States. Although diplomatic relations between the two countries were originally established in 1965, the Canadian embassy in Damascus did not open until 1985. Syria, however, did not open its embassy in Ottawa, Canada, until 1999. In recent years, political relations between Syria and Canada have been cemented with a series of visits by leaders. Former Canadian foreign ministers Lloyd Axworthy and John Manley visited Syria in November 1997, June 2000, and October 2001. Canadian defense minister Art Eggleton visited in September 1999. A higher level visit to Damascus was made by Canadian prime minister Jean Chrétien in April 2000. Syrian foreign minister Faruq al-Shara'a made an official visit to Ottawa in June 1999.

Further improvement in political relations between Syria and Canada is expected as a result of reforms being made by the new Syrian leadership. These changes have led to an expansion in cultural and social activities. Recent projects include the opening of Canadian Education Resource Centers at the universities in Damascus and Aleppo. Canada's Quebec City also held a major exhibition of Syrian artifacts, entitled "Syria: Land of Civilization," in May 2000.

Left: **Syria and Canada enjoy good diplomatic relations. In April 2000, Canada's prime minister, Jean Chrétien, visited Damascus during his tour of the Middle East.**

Trade Between Syria and Canada

Canada and Syria have a trade imbalance. Canada imports more goods from Syria than it exports to the country. Between 1995 and 2001, Canadian exports to Syria were worth CAN $21 million annually and included wooden poles, aluminum, mechanical and electrical equipment, and textiles. In the same timeframe, imports from Syria had risen drastically from CAN $27 million to CAN $61 million annually. The main Syrian product imported to Canada was crude oil, which accounted for CAN $43 million. Other key items included cotton T-shirts and fruit products. Canada has had a multi-year textile agreement with Syria.

Canadian companies such as Tanganyika Oil Company, Titan Engineering, and Macdonald Engineering play an active role in Syria's oil and gas industries. The petroleum industry in Syria has much potential, and Canada provides technical expertise to Syrian petroleum companies. Canadian companies are also active in Syria's agricultural sector, to which they supply machinery, fertilizers, livestock, and genetic material. Agriculture accounts for over 50 percent of economic activity in Syria's private sector.

Above: **Canada-based companies continue to invest in Syria. These workers are building a new Four Seasons Hotel in Damascus.**

Easing of Restrictions

Since President Bashar al-Assad took office, he has introduced a number of reforms that will lift restrictions on trade between Syria and Canada as well as with the rest of the world. Laws have also been introduced to encourage foreigners to invest in Syria's agricultural, banking, industrial, and tourism sectors. Some Canadian companies with a business presence in Syria include Air Canada, BA Banknote, Canadair, Royal Canadian Mint, SNC Lavalin, and Stella Jones. Other Canadian businesses are also looking to forge links with Syrian companies. Their areas of interest are in business machinery, energy and power, telecommunications, information science, and transportation.

Tourism in Syria

Despite its shaky political situation, tourists from both Canada and the United States are still drawn to Syria. This may be because of Syria's wealth of tourist attractions and the great sense of history that pervades the area.

Below: **Although Syria is not known for being a major tourist center, visitors to the country are attracted by both its historical ruins and its beautiful beaches.**

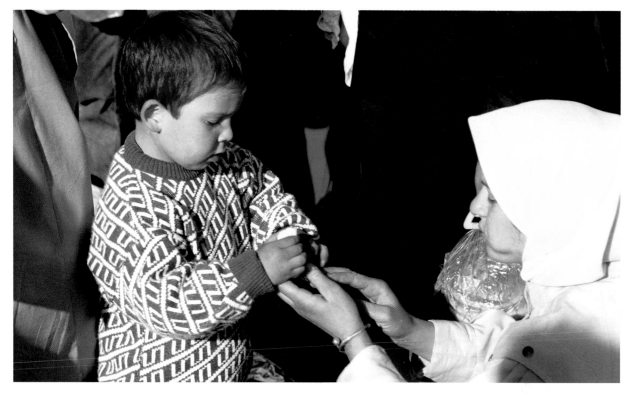

Development Agencies

Canada contributes funds to several organizations that are active in Syria. Most of these organizations are part of the United Nations and include the United Nations Relief and Works Agency for Palestine Refugees in the Near East (UNRWA), United Nations Children's Fund (UNICEF), United Nations Development Program (UNDP), and the UN Truce Supervision Organization (UNTSO). Canada has also participated in the UN Disengagement Observer Force in the Golan Heights (UNDOF) since 1974 and has military personnel stationed in the area.

Above: International agencies such as UNICEF operate a number of programs in Syria. Their services include setting up family meeting centers for divorced parents as well as getting more girls to attend school.

Syrian Community Center of Canada

Members of the Syrian community in Canada have strong ties with their homeland and with each other. The Web site of the Syrian Community Center of Canada provides information for Syrians coming to Canada and for Canadians wishing either to visit Syria or to seek business contacts in Syria. The members of the center integrate their Syrian heritage into their new home in Canada and help other members contribute to their new community and country. In addition, they are also committed to informing Canadians about the culture, language, and heritage of Syria.

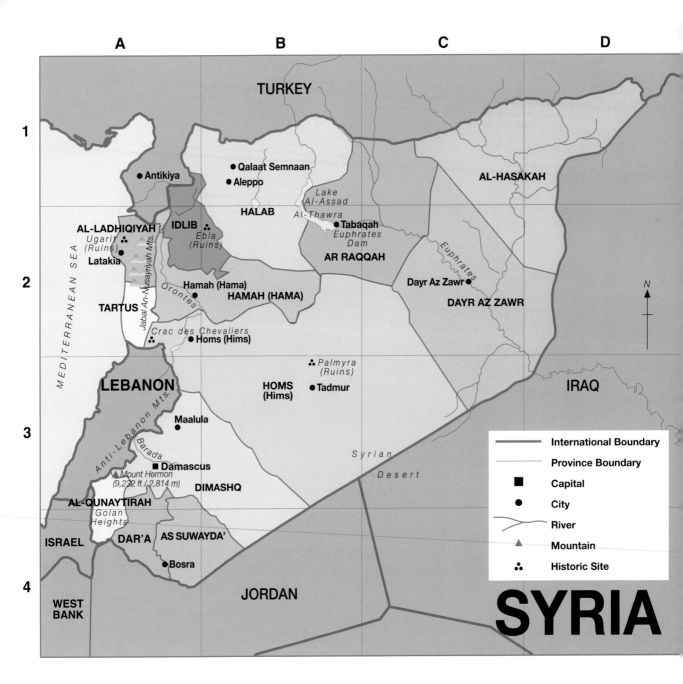

Map labels (reading the map):

A   **B**   **C**   **D**

1

TURKEY

● Antikiya

● Qalaat Semnaan

● Aleppo

AL-HASAKAH

AL-LADHIQIYAH

IDLIB

Lake Al-Assad

Al-Thawra

Ugarit
(Ruins)

HALAB

Ebla
(Ruins)

● Tabaqah
*Euphrates
Dam*

● Latakia

Euphrates

2

MEDITERRANEAN SEA

Jabal An-Nusayriyah Mts.

AR RAQQAH

Hamah (Hama) ●

● Dayr Az Zawr

TARTUS

Orontes

HAMAH (HAMA)

DAYR AZ ZAWR

Crac des Chevaliers

● Homs (Hims)

*Palmyra
(Ruins)*

3

LEBANON

HOMS
(Hims)

● Tadmur

IRAQ

Anti-Lebanon Mts.

Lebanon Mts.

● Maalula

Syrian

Desert

Barada

■ Damascus

▲ Mount Hermon
(9,232 ft / 2,814 m)

AL-QUNAYTIRAH

DIMASHQ

Golan
Heights

ISRAEL

DAR'A

AS SUWAYDA'

4

WEST
BANK

● Bosra

JORDAN

SYRIA

Legend:

———	International Boundary
———	Province Boundary
■	Capital
●	City
～	River
▲	Mountain
⁂	Historic Site

86

Above: Visitors to the Omayyad Mosque in Damascus are often amazed at the beautiful facade.

Al-Thawra B2
Al Hasakah (province) C1–D2
Al-Ladhiqiyah (province) A2
Al-Qunaytirah (province) A3
Aleppo B1
Antikiya A1
Ar Raqqah (province) B1–C2
As Suwayda' (province) A3–B3

Barada River A3
Bosra A4

Crac des Chevaliers A2

Damascus A3
Dar'a (province) A3–A4
Dayr az Zawr (city) C2
Dayr az Zawr (province) C2

Dimashq (province) A3–B3

Ebla B2
Euphrates Dam B2
Euphrates River B1–C2

Golan Heights A4

Halab (province) B1–B2
Hamah (city) A2
Hamah (province) A2–B2
Homs (city) A2
Homs (province) A2–C3

Idlib (province) A1–B2
Iraq C3–D1
Israel A3–A4

Jabal an-Nusayriyah A2
Jordan A4–B4

Lake Al-Assad B1–B2
Latakia A2
Lebanon A3

Maalula A3
Mediterranean Sea A1–A3
Mount Hermon A3

Orontes River A2

Palmyra B3

Qalaat Semaan B1

Syrian Desert B3–C3

Tabaqah B2
Tadmur B3
Tartus (province) A2
Turkey A1–D1

Ugarit A2

West Bank A4

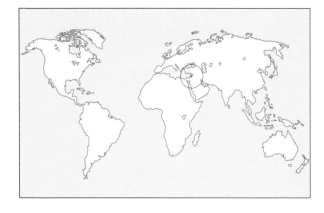

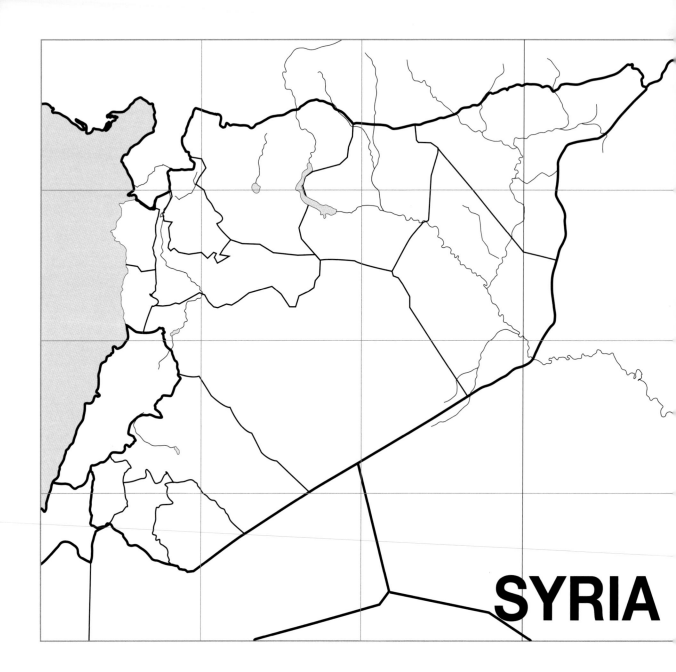

SYRIA

How Is Your Geography?

Learning to identify the main geographical areas and points of a country can be challenging. Although it may seem difficult at first to memorize the locations and spellings of major cities or the names of mountain ranges, rivers, deserts, lakes, and other prominent physical features, the end result of this effort can be very rewarding. Places you previously did not know existed will suddenly come to life when referred to in world news, whether in newspapers, television reports, other books and reference sources, or on the Internet. This knowledge will make you feel a bit closer to the rest of the world, with its fascinating variety of cultures and physical geography.

This map can be duplicated for use in a classroom. (PLEASE DO NOT WRITE IN THIS BOOK!) Students can then fill in any requested information on their individual map copies. The student can also make a copy of the map and use it as a study tool to practice indentifying place names and geographical features on his or her own.

Above: Souks are a great place to shop. This souk in Aleppo is devoted to the textile industry.

Syria at a Glance

Official Name	Syrian Arab Republic
Capital	Damascus
Official Language	Arabic
Population	17,585,540 (July 2002 estimate)
Land area	71,479 square miles (185,180 square kilometers)
Provinces	Al-Hasakah, Al-Ladhiqiyah, Al-Qunaytirah, Ar Raqqah, As Suwayda', Dar'a, Dayr az Zawr, Dimashq, Halab, Hamah (Hama), Homs (Hims), Idlib, and Tartus
Lowest point	Unnamed location near Lake Tiberias 656 ft (200 m) below sea level, in the contested Golan Heights
Highest point	Mount Hermon 9,232 feet (2,814 meters)
Coastline	120 miles (193 km)
Border countries	Iraq, Israel, Jordan, Lebanon, Turkey
Major Rivers	Euphrates, Orontes
Major Cities	Aleppo, Hamah, Homs, Latakia
Religion	Islam, Christianity
Head of State	Bashar al-Assad (since July 17, 2000)
Holidays	New Year's Day (January 1), Revolution Day (March 8), Mother's Day (March 21), Independence Day (April 17), Labor Day (May 1), Martyrs' Day (May 6), Christmas (December 25)
Major Festivals	Easter, Eid al-Fitr, Eid al-Adha, Prophet Muhammad's Birthday
Exports	crude oil, petroleum products, fruits and vegetables, cotton fiber, clothing, meat, and live animals
Imports	machinery and transportation equipment, food and livestock, metals and metal products, chemicals and chemical products
Currency	Syrian Pound (1 SYP = U.S. $0.021 as of 2004)

Opposite: **A partial view of the Great Mosque at Aleppo is visible through a doorway in the citadel.**

Glossary

Arabic Vocabulary

al-manqal (al-MAN-kal): a barbecue set.

baba ghanoush (BA-ba ga-NOOJ): a dip made from sesame paste and baked eggplant, usually eaten with bread.

Bilad al Sham (bi-LAD uh-SHAM): the collective name given to modern-day Jordan, Syria, Lebanon, and Israel prior to World War I.

bismillah (bis-ME-lah): literally in the name of God.

bulgar (BUL-gah): processed wheat which has been boiled, dried, and crushed.

debke (dib-KE): a traditional folk dance.

Eid al-Adha (EED al-AD-ha): the Islamic feast of sacrifice.

Eid al-Fitr (EED al-FIT-er): a three-day feast held at the end of Ramadan.

fahm (FA-him): charcoal.

fajr (FAJ): the dawn prayer or first prayer of the day for Muslims.

hajj (HAJ): the Muslim pilgrimage to the holy city of Mecca, which every believer tries to visit at least once in their life.

hammam (HAM-mum): a public bathhouse.

iftar (if-TAR): the meal eaten to break the fast during the month of Ramadan.

isha (i-SHA): the night prayer or fifth prayer of the day for Muslims.

maghrib (magh-RIB): the evening prayer or fourth prayer of the day for Muslims.

Majlis al-Shaab (MAJ-lis a-SHAAB): the legislative branch of the government in Syria, also called the People's Council.

mahr (MAR): money or goods given to the bride's family by the groom or his family.

mezze (me-ZIH): appetizers or little dishes that are often eaten with bread in Syria.

muhafazah (mu-HAF-az-ah): a province or an administrative unit of the country.

noria (NO-ria): a giant waterwheel.

qamareddine (kumm-er-i-DEEN): an apricot drink made by adding boiling water to small pieces of apricot paste.

sahur (sa-HER): a light meal eaten by Muslims before the dawn prayer.

sawm (SOWM): the act of fasting from sunrise to sundown for Muslims.

shahada (sah-HAH-dah): the prayer that says that Muslims believe there is no god but Allah and Muhammad is Allah's prophet.

shari'a (shah-REE-ah): Islamic law.

tarawih (ta-ra-WEEH): a night prayer said by Muslims during Ramadan.

English Vocabulary

archaeologists: a person who studies the artifacts and remains of ancient people in order to learn about their culture.

breeding: the act of keeping animals so as to produce more offspring.

brocade: a type of fabric that is often woven using gold or silver thread.

caliph: a title for a leader in Islam.

cardamon: a type of spice used for cooking in the Middle East.

coup: to overthrow or attempt a takeover of the government by violent means.

curriculum: the courses studied in school.

damask: an elaborately patterned fabric.

deciphering: to make out the meaning.

desertification: the process by which an area becomes a desert.

dissent: to have a different opinion.

dwindled: to become lesser in quantity.

eclipsed: to block out or overshadow.

embroidery: the art of sewing beautiful patterns onto cloth by needlework.

encroachment: to have extended beyond the usual boundary.

excavation: to dig in the ground; part of an archaeological site where objects are being dug up.

excel: to do better than others.

extensive: covering a large area.

flamboyant: very grand and elaborate.

flintlock: part of a gun commonly used in the seventeenth century.

foals: the young of a horse.

fortification: to add elements to strengthen the original structure.

humanitarian: a person working to improve the welfare and happiness of others.

impregnable: strong enough to resist or withstand attack.

inauguration: the day on which something officially starts.

indigenous: native to a particular place.

infiltrated: to pass as a member of a group by untruthful means.

initiated: introduced or started.

insignificant: of no importance.

insubordination: disobedient, not submitting to authority.

intarsia: the art of decorating a wooden surface with inlaid patterns.

intrinsic: that which is already belonging to a thing by virtue of its nature.

legacy: a gift or skill that is passed down from one's ancestors.

mandate: the authority given to a nation to rule and govern another country.

monumental: exceptionally great.

navigable: water that is deep and wide enough to allow ships to pass through.

obsession: an idea, image, object, or person that is constantly in one's thoughts.

ornamented: a design which is added in order to make something more attractive.

outpost: a station or settlement of a country in a foreign land.

patriarchal: relating to a society where fathers are the head of the family, with property only passing to male heirs.

picturesque: a charming picture or scene.

prosperity: a period of good fortune.

prototype: the original or model on which something is based.

Ramadan: the ninth month of the Islamic calendar during which all eligible Muslims fast from sunrise to sunset.

relinquished: to surrender, give up, or let go of a claim to something.

revolution: to replace a government or political system by force.

salinity: the amount of salt content.

salvaging: to save or rescue anything from danger or destruction.

seclusion: removed or separated from the general public.

secular: that which is related to worldly things; not of a religious nature.

souk: a traditional marketplace specializing in one type of product.

suspended: to stop or postpone.

tremendously: of great amount or size.

undulating: a surface which rises and falls.

unicameral: a government which consists of a single chamber or house.

More Books to Read

The Arab-Israeli Conflict. Tony McAleavy (SIGS Books and Multimedia)

Eyewitness: Islam. Eyewitness Books series. Philip Wilkinson (Dorling Kindersley)

Hand Full of Stars. Rafik Schami (Puffin Books)

A Historical Atlas of Syria. Alison Stark Draper (Rosen)

Mesopotamia. Cultures of the Past series. Pamela F. Service (Benchmark Books)

The Middle East. Auriana Ojeda (editor) (Greenhaven Press)

Mosque. David Macaulay (Houghton Mifflin)

The Ottoman Empire. Cultures of the Past series. Adriane Ruggiero (Benchmark Books)

Saladin: Noble Prince of Islam. Diane Stanley (Harpercollins)

Syria. Fiesta! series. (Grolier Educational)

Syria. Major World Nations series. Martin Mulloy (Chelsea House)

The Tigris and Euphrates Rivers. Watts Library series. Melissa Whitcraft (Franklin Watts)

Videos

The 50 Years War: Israel and the Arabs. (PBS Home Video)

Islam: Empire of Faith. (PBS Home Video)

Lost Worlds of the Middle East: Syria, Jordan, Lebanon, Israel. Director, Rick Ray.

The Middle East and Central Asia: Land and Resources. (AIMS Multimedia)

Travel the World by Train: Near & Middle East. (Pioneer Video)

Web Sites

www.academickids.com/world/geos/sy.html

www.state.gov/p/nea/ci/c2420.htm

www.worldalmanacforkids.com/explore/nations/syria.html

Due to the dynamic nature of the Internet, some web sites stay current longer than others. To find additional web sites, use a reliable search engine with one or more of the following keywords to help you locate information about Syria. Keywords: *Aleppo, Damascus, Euphrates, Golan Heights, Mount Hermon, Omayyad Mosque, Palmyra.*

Index